# 4500

# *BABY NAMES*

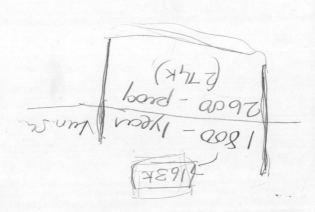

# *4500 BABY NAMES*

*Shashi Jain*

Published by:

**GOODWILL PUBLISHING HOUSE**

B-3 Rattan Jyoti, 18 Rajendra Place
New Delhi (India)
Tel.: 25750801, 25820556
Fax: 91-11-25764396
E-mail: goodwillpub@vsnl.net
website: www.goodwillpublishinghouse.com
Printed by: G.S. Enterprises

**GOODWILL PUBLISHING HOUSE®**
B-3 RATTAN JYOTI, 18 RAJENDRA PLACE
NEW DELHI -110008 (INDIA)

© Publishers

*Published by*
**GOODWILL PUBLISHING HOUSE®**
B-3 Rattan Jyoti, 18 Rajendra Place
New Delhi-110008 (INDIA)
Tel. : 25750801, 25820556
Fax : 91-11-25764396
E-mail : goodwillpub@vsnl.net
website : www.goodwillpublishinghouse.com
Printed by G. S. Enterprises

# <u>Introduction</u>

Name is the first identity of a person. Without a name one is nobody. Even pet animals do have names and they respond to it. It is an expression of distinction, love and importance for everyone. The name evokes certain quality and uniqueness. No tribe, civilization and culture can be found on the earth without a name of the individuals.

There can be several ways to name a baby.

It can be a combination of parental name.

It can be a named after a God, Goddess or deity.

A name can be derived from the epics and religious source.

A name can be after an idol or ideal, be it a historical figure, king, leader, religious or cult-figure, a musician, poet, writer or a film star.

A name can be based upon alphabetical preference, and sometimes on astrological calculations.

A name can be given on the basis of phonetic rhythm or just for the beauty of letters or word.

Sometimes names are given after the planet, star, river, mountain, state, city, village and other geographical expressions.

A name may also reflect a flower, park, tree, precious stone, metal and other natural phenomenon.

It is also common to find the name representing the occupation and profession.

The name can be symbiotic of the dynasty, lineage or special characteristics of a family, like secraments, caste, education, wealth, etc.

One can also come across the names having strange meanings and unexpected sources.

Names are also kept on the basis of numerology and it is a common practice to give 1 to 9 numbers in the order of A to

I and the cycle continuous upto 'Z' (26, i.e. $2 + 6 = 8$). All the letters are added according to their numerical value (from 1 to 9). The number of the owner indicates owner's planet, character and future.

Names are given commonly to identify a person on the basis of his or her complexion, special features, physique and personality. Particularly for girls, it is common to express her beauty through the name.

In the countries with long history and rich cultural background, like India, particular attention is given that a name is solemn and sacred. Its etymology and pronunciation must be auspicious and bring glory, logentivity, prosperity and luck. This is the reason that most of the names are still given after the gods and goddesses.

The name often reflects the aspirations and wish of the parents. It is for the child to stand upto the expectation for which all the parents put in their best efforts. Conversely, it is also true that the name gives a psychological image to the owner as well as to others and often a name moulds a person bearing it. Selecting a name for a baby needs utmost care, sensitivity and holistic considerations. It must be remembered that such considerations often cross the barriers of science and logic. They have their roots in emotional, mystique and spiritual beliefs. No doubt, highly educated parents often consult the astrologers, uneducated elders in the family and godman. And they are not wrong.

A name is not simply a word or just the letters. It is an image. Every name, whether Ram, Savitri, Mohammed or Amitabh, evokes a particular image. It leaves certain impression on the mind. The image that a name creates may not be the same for everyone. It depends upon one's background, perceptions, knowledge and personal experience.

Like Hindu Vedas speak of "Namkaran Sanskar", every religion and culture identifies naming ceremony as sacred. The divinities associated with fertility, prosperity and well being are invoked, Mantras are uttered, the elders and knowledgeable revered and the poor are fed. Prayers are made so that the family tree is blessed with health, wealth and fame. The Namkaran ceremony is normally performed on the tenth or twelfth day after birth.

It is really difficult to select a name for a new-born among so many. There are some tips, which may be useful in this task.

The name should be simple, short and sweet.

It should have rhythm and should be easy to pronounce. Repitition of first letter in surname or second name provides harmony, e.g. Ram, Rehman, Raj, Rewal, Charles, Correa, etc.

Avoid unfashionable words. Nowadays the middle name looks outdated.

The name should not be too common. Search for a little unusual name, so that the child stands out of the crowd.

Avoid names after rivers, mountains and other geographical features. These are not considered auspicious.

Names with even number of letters (2, 4 & 6) appear suitable for males, while with uneven numbers (3 & 5) look feminine, thus suitable for females.

Male names should not end with 'e' (i), otherwise they sound feminine. Feminine names expressing beauty and elegance are always refreshing (for example, Padmini, Ragini, Suhasini, etc.)

So go ahead and choose a beautiful name for your love.

**Shashi Jain**

# Names for Baby Boy

# A

**Abharan** – covering
**Abhas** – awareness
**Adarsh** – looking glass
**Adrsh** – ideal
**Adhikar** – Lord Shiva
**Adideva** – God
**Adinath** – the first tirthankar of Jains
**Adishwara** – king
**Adisur** – king
**Adita** – from the fish
**Aditaya** – immortal
**Adityesha** – Sun God
**Agneya** – son of Agni Deva
**Akar** – shape
**Akarsh** – to attract
**Akarshan** – attracted
**Akash** – sky
**Akash Deep** – light of sky

**Alaap** – first part of music
**Alok** – cry of victory
**Amod** – joy
**Anand** – joy
**Anadmaya** – deeply happy
**Anandgiri** – mountain of happiness
**Anand-Murti** – picture of joy
**Anand Rupa** – eternal joy
**Ashitendu** – one who is satisfied after having food
**Ashish** – blessed
**Ashutosh** – one who is easily pleased
**Ashtika** – one who has faith in Vedas
**Atma Chand** – Moon soul

**Atma Ram** – to get spritual knowledge

**Atma Nand** – one who win himself

**Atmaja** – born to one-self

**Atmiya** – a person who is near to you

**Ayati** – magestic

**Abhaya** – fearless

**Abhi Chandra** – Lord Krishna, an auspicious time

**Abhijaya** – one who is victorious

**Abhijita** – victorious

**Abhijata** – a sage

**Abheeka** – lover

**Abhilasha** – desire

**Abhimanee** – proud

**Abhimanyu** – son of Arjuna, quick to anger

**Abhinandana** – to greet

**Abhinava** – new

**Abhiratha** – great charioteer

**Abhirupa** – pleasing

**Abhisheka** – ceremonial bath

**Abhivandana** – to salute

**Abhra** – a cloud

**Abhyudaya** – risen to prosperity

**Achala** – one who is firm

**Achalandra** – king of mountain

**Achyuta** – imperishable, Lord Vishnu

**Achyuta Nandaya** – the joy of remaining imperishable

**Achyuta Vikranta** – courageous

**Adhara** – beneath

**Adheesha** – emperor

**Adhideva** – highest God

**Adhila** – sincere

**Aditya** – a sage

**Adri** – mountain

**Adavya** – unique

**Aftab** – fire, Sun

**Agendra** – king of mountain

**Agnajita** – conqueror of fire

**Agnika** – related to fire

**Agniprava** – lustrous like fire

**Agrima** – leader

**Ahernisha** – day and night

**Ajaata** – unborn

**Ajaya** – always victorious

**Ajitaabha** – conqueror of sky

**Ajita** – invincible

**Ajitesha** – Vishnu

**Ajmala** – picious man

**Ajneya** – the unknown

**Akhilesha** – the almighty

**Akhila** – the whole

**Akrura** – not cruel

**Akshana** – eye

**Akshara** – imperishable

**Akshata** – the whole, unbroken rice used for worship

**Akshaya** – indestructable

**Akshina** – infallible

**Akshit** – permanent

**Akopa** – a person who does not get angry easily

**Akula** – Lord Shiva

**Alankara** – decoration

**Alankrita** – decorated

**Aloka** – man with lovely hair

**Aloke** – light

**Alpesha** – smaller than an atom

**Aman** – peace

**Amar** – a person who never dies

**Amarjeet** – winner of the death

**Amarisha** – Lord Indra
**Ambara** – the sky
**Ambdhi** – the ocean
**Ambrisha** – Lord Vishnu
**Ampuja** – the lotus
**Ameeta** – unlimited
**Amer** – name of a king
**Amteshvara** – enternal God
**Amita** – without limit
**Amitabha** – lustrous
**Amitav** – name of Lord Buddha
**Amitatma** – devine soul
**Amitesha** – infinite God
**Amrita** – nectar
**Amritanshu** – drop of nectar
**Amoda** – pleasure
**Amogha** – successful
**Amola** – priceless
**Amoghsiddhi** – one who does not fail

**Anada** – eternal
**Anagha** – innocent
**Anamitra** – the Sun
**Anamol** – invaluable
**Ananga** – Kamdev
**Anala** – God for fire
**Ananta** – infinite
**Ananantdeva** – eternal God
**Anantashisha** – a person having countless heads
**Anchala** – the decorative end of sari
**Anchita** – honoured
**Angada** – bracelet, son of Bali
**Angaj** – produced from the body
**Aniketa** – homeless
**Animisha** – a unwinkable
**Anirjita** – unconquerable
**Anirudh** – a person who coperates without any hurdle

**Anirvana** – undying
**Anisha** – life without darkness, Lord Vishnu
**Anjali** – a hollow formed by joining two hands
**Anjalika** – small house
**Ankita** – marked
**Ankur** – off shoot
**Anmola** – invaluable, priceless
**Ananta** – eternal
**Anoop** – graceful
**Anshu** – minute particle
**Anshuka** – muslim
**Anshul** – radiant
**Anshumana** – the Sun
**Antariksha** – the space
**Anubhava** – experience
**Anugra** – calm
**Anuja** – younger

**Anukampa** – gratitude
**Anunanya** – pray
**Anup** – pond
**Anupam** – excellent
**Anuraaga** – devotion
**Anurakta** – devoted
**Anuttama** – best of all
**Anuvinda** – one who has obtained
**Apara** – too much
**Aparjita** – undefeated
**Apoorve** – beautiful
**Archana** – worship
**Archita** – worshipped
**Ardhendu** – half Moon
**Arhanta** – destroyer of enemies
**Arjita** – earned
**Arjuna** – peacook, spotless white
**Arka** – Sun
**Arnava** – ocean
**Arnesha** – Lord of the sea

**Arun** – the dawn

**Arvinda** – lotus

**Aasamana** – sky

**Ashesha** – entire

**Ashanka** – feerless

**Asananda** – hopeful

**Aseema** – limitless

**Asita** – not white

**Ashok** – without grief

**Ashutosh** – Shiva

**Ashwini** – a star, a cavalier

**Atal** – immovable

**Atma** – soul

**Atmaja** – a son

**Atmanand** – bliss of soul

**Atula** – matchless

**Atulya** – matchless

**Avani** – Earth

**Avanindra** – Lord of the Earth

**Avanish** – Lord of the Earth

**Avanti** – name of the city

**Avinash** – understructable

**Avishkaar** – new invention

**Avkasha** – Limitless space

**Avatara** – incarnation

**Ayodhya Natha** – Lord Rama

**Ayushya** – life time

**Azima** – one who is destines

# B

**Badal** – cloud
**Badri** – Lord Vishnu
**Badrinarayan** – Narayan of Badri
**Badrinatha** – Lord Vishnu
**Bahul** – a star
**Bahubali** – a jain tirthankar
**Bajrang** – name of Hanuman
**Balbir** – a person with strength
**Baldeva** – a strong person
**Balendu** – the new Moon
**Balraj** – a valourous person
**Balsudan** – one who has power to hurt
**Balvant** – a person with strength
**Balvindra** – brave

**Badhula** – pleasing
**Banarsi** – a person residing in Banaras
**Bannishikha** – flame
**Bansi** – flute
**Bankim** – curved
**Bankim Chand** – curved Moon
**Bansila** – Lord Krishna
**Basanta** – the spring season
**Basu** – one who is wealthy
**Bhadra** – gentle
**Bhadrajeeta** – one who is victorious
**Bhadraprana** – tree with beautiful leaves
**Bhagvata** – religious
**Bhagirath** – who bought Ganga to Earth

**Bhagvaticharan** – at the feet of goddess

**Bhagvati Prasad** – gift of goddess

**Bhagvati** – God

**Bhagwant** – God

**Bhagvant Singh** – fortunate

**Bhagya** – fortune

**Bhagyaraja** – Lord or fortune

**Bhairav** – Lord shiva

**Bhajan** – worship

**Bhakta** – devotee

**Bhanu** – Sun

**Bhanudya** – rising Sun

**Bhanudasa** – devotee of Sun

**Bharata** – India, son of Shakuntla

**Bharania** – constatellation

**Bhaskara** – Sun

**Bhashanatar** – linguistic disparities

**Bhashaya** – spoken words

**Bhavbhuti** – ashes of Shiva

**Bhavishya** – future

**Bhavitya** – an incident which is going to happen

**Bhavajan** – one who has knowledge of the world

**Bhaumika** – pertains to Earth

**Bhavesha** – Lord of the world

**Bhavya** – good featured

**Bhima** – second Pandu son

**Bhimsen** – fearful

**Bhisham** – strong, unbreakable

**Bhushan** – ornaments

**Bhukhand** – part of the land

# C

**Chaitanya** – knowledge, awareness spirit, vitality

**Chaitra** – name of lunar month

**Chaitrasakha** – God of love

**Chaitrartha** – Kuber's garden

**Chakora** – alert, bird

**Chakaradhara** – Lord Vishnu

**Chakrapani** – Lord Vishnu

**Chakshu** – eyes

**Chakshusha** – related to eyes

**Chakrang** – swan

**Chakrayudh** – Lord Vishnu

**Chalukya** – an ancient God

**Chaman** – a garden

**Chamanlal** – a small garden

**Chaanaaksha** – clever

**Chanchala** – not steady

**Chanchu** – clever

**Chandbhanu** – the Sun

**Chandbhargava** – Shiva in his terrible form

**Chanda** – the Moon

**Chandan** – Malayachal mountain

**Chandangiri** – sandal wood

**Chandak** – the Moon

**Chandeesha** – Lord Shiva

**Chandeshvara** – Lord Shiva

**Chandavikrama** – fierce

**Chandodeva** – the Moon

**Chandra** – the Moon, glittering

**Chandra Bandhu** – kumud flower

**Chandra Kumar** – son of Moon

**Chandra Chuda** – Lord Shiva

**Chandradatta** – Moon gifted

**Chandrahaasa** – the bow of Lord Shiva

**Chandrajeet** – conqueror of Moon

**Chandraki** – peacock

**Chandra Madhava** – Moon honey

**Chandra Mohan** – attractive like Moon

**Chandra Mauli** – Lord Shiva

**Chandra Mukta** – Lord Shiva

**Chandrankita** – Lord Shiva

**Chandrashu** – Lord Vishnu

**Chandra Prakash** – Moonlight

**Chandra Shekhara** – crested Moon

**Chandrasana** – face like Moon

**Chandra Saurbha** – as famous as Moon

**Chandrayana** – the path of the Moon

**Chandresha** – king of the Moon

**Chandrila** – Lord Shiva

**Chandra Varmana** – brave like Moon

**Channa** – well known

**Chandrika** – Moon light

**Chandrama** – Moon

**Chappal** – not steady, active

**Chaanakya** – Prime-minister of Chandra Gupta

**Charana** – support, feet

**Charanjeeta** – one who over the Lord

**Chatur** – clever

**Chaturabhuja** – one with four arms

**Chaturamukha** – one with four face

**Chetana** – supreme soul

**Chetanananda** – supreme joy

**Chhatra** – an umbrella

**Chhatrapati** – a sovereign king

**Chhandaka** – Lord Vishnu

**Chhaila** – handsome young man

**Chhayanka** – the Moon

**Chhanyankara** – the bearer of an umbrella

**Chhayatanya** – son of Chhaya

**Chhayanatha** – Lord of shadow

**Chidambra** – one whose heart is as large as sky

**Chidakasha** – one whose heart is as large as sky

**Chiddnanda** – Lord Shiva

**Chidarupa** – to incarnate knowledge

**Chinmaya** – blissful

**Chintak** – the intellectual

**Chintana** – meditation

**Chintamani** – the stone of the philosopher

**Chiraga** – lamp

**Chiranjeevaa** – long life

**Chirantana** – ancient

**Chitranga** – Arjun

**Chitravesha** – with extra ordinary dress

**Chitrabhanu** – Sun

**Chitraketu** – name of king of Gandharva

**Chitrangada** – a son of Shatanshu

**Chitrarthi** – having a beautiful chariot

**Chitrasena** – gandharva king

**Chitroopa** – with beautiful form

**Chitt** – mind

**Chittranyan** – joy of inner mind

**Chittranjana** – one who pleases the mind

**Chittesha** – Lord of the soul

**Chittswaroop** – like a God

**Chittvana** – one who meditates

**Chuddamani** – crest jewel

**Cuddaratha** – crest jewel

# D

**Dadheechi** – name of a sage

**Daksha** – expert, competent, clever

**Dakshesha** – Lord Shiva

**Dakshpati** – Lord of the faculties (Shiva)

**Dakshina** – south, competent

**Dakshinamoorti** – Lord Shiva

**Dakshya** – panini, the sage

**Dama** – a son

**Damachandra** – supressor of Moon

**Damaghosha** – father of Shishupal of Mahabharata

**Damana** – subdued

**Damodara** – Shri Krishna

**Dandanayaka** – Head Magistrate

**Dandin** – a Brahmin of the fourth order

**Daanveera** – very generous

**Dantadhvaja** – name of Rishi

**Dard** – ocean

**Dariyahala** – son of the sea

**Darpaka** – Kamdev

**Darpana** – mirror

**Darpita** – proud

**Daruk** – Vishnu

**Darshanlal** – beauty, sight

**Daruka** – deodar tree

**Dashabala** – possessor of ten power

**Dashabahu** – Lord Shiva

**Dashamaya** – rudra
**Dashashava** – Moon
**Dasharashmi** – the Sun
**Dashasheesha** – Ravana, ten headed
**Dasharatha** – a king of Ayodhya
**Datrim** – got from God as a favour
**Dattachitt** – one who is engrossed in giving
**Dayaal** – generous
**Dayalchanda** – generous Moon
**Dayakar** – Lord Shiva
**Dayakut** – Lord Buddha
**Dayamaya** – kind person
**Dayananda** – one who is kind hearted
**Dayanidhi** – pity, mercy
**Dayarama** – Ram, the merciful

**Dayasaagar** – full of compassion
**Dayashankara** – merciful Shankar
**Dayavanta** – enerous
**Dayita** – beloved
**Debashisha** – blessing of God
**Deenbandhu** – brother of poor
**Deendayal** – merciful for poor
**Deenanatha** – Lord of poor
**Deep** – lamp
**Deepmay** – lustrous
**Deepak** – lamp
**Deepankara** – flame of lamp
**Deepaayana** – pathway of a lamp
**Deependra** – Lord of the light
**Deepesha** – Lord of light
**Deeptanga** – peacock
**Deeptanshu** – Sun
**Deeptendu** – Moon

**Deeptiketu** – light bannered

**Deva** – God

**Devadasa** – follower of God

**Devadatta** – name of Arjun's conch-shell

**Devadeepa** – divine light of the lamp

**Devajyoti** – lustre of God

**Devagiri** – mountains of God

**Devamani** – jewel of Vishnu

**Devapriya** – dear to God

**Devashree** – fate, fortune

**Devesha** – Lord Indra

**Deveshwara** – Lord Shiva

**Devendra** – king of Angels, Lord Indra

**Devilal** – son of Devi

**Devishaya** – whose protector is Devi

**Dhaareshwar** – king Bhoja

**Dhairyavana** – one who is courageous

**Dhananjaya** – Arjun, Agni

**Dhana** – property, wealth

**Dhanaman** – name of the king

**Dhanamani** – jewel of wealth

**Dhanapati** – Lord of the wealth

**Dhanesha** – Lord of the wealth

**Dhanika** – rich, wealthy

**Dhanurdhara** – bearer of the bows

**Dhanvantri** – the author of Ayurveda

**Dhanvin** – armed with bow

**Dharma** – religion, duty

**Dharmaditya** – a name of Buddha

**Dharmananda** – religious person

**Dharmanetra** – eye of justice

**Dharmaprabhasha** – illumination of justice

**Dharmavarmana** – Lord Krishna

**Dharmesha** – Lord of justice

**Dharmendra** – Lord Indra

**Dharmeshawara** – Lord of justice

**Dhatrim** – got from

**Dhritaketu** – firm, bannered

**Dhritrashtra** – Kuru king

**Dhrupada** – father of Dropadi

**Dhrusudhumn** – brother of Dropadi

**Dhruva** – a star in the space

**Dhyaneshwara** – master of meditation

**Didhya** – sky

**Diganta** – end of the horizon

**Digvijaya** – conquest in all directions

**Dinakant** – Sun

**Dinakar** – Sun

**Dilip** – a lustrous king of Ishvaku dynesty

**Dilwara** – brave

**Dinagam** – the down

**Diner** – the Sun

**Dinesh** – Sun

**Dineshwara** – the Sun

**Dipt** – full of light

**Diptmana** – famous

**Dishanta** – yagya performed to bring peace

**Disht** – fortune

**Divakara** – the Sun

**Divaspati** – Lord Indra

**Divij** – the Angel

**Divraj** – Indra

**Divij** – born in heaven

**Diviyaanga** – divine, heavenly

**Divy** – radiant

**Divyankshu** – divine eyes

**Divyaman** – the Sun

**Divyaprakash** – celestial light

**Divyendu** – bright Moon

**Divyodak** – rain water

**Diyanshu** – the Sun

**Dooshana** – a general of Ravana

**Dristivanta** – learned man

**Dristavya** – worth seeing

**Drutivant** – handsome

**Dronacharya** – name of guru of Kauravas and Pandavas

**Durgesha** – Lord Shiva

**Dushala** – brother of Duryodhana

**Dushaasan** – brother of Duryodhana

**Duryodhana** – son of Dhritrashtra

**Durvasaa** – name of Rishi

**Dushyant** – destroyer of evil

**Dwarkaadheesha** – Lord Krishna

**Dwarkanatha** – Lord Krishna

**Dwij** – twice born

**Dwijpati** – Moon, brahmin

**Dwaipaayana** – name of Vyasa Rishi

**Dwipendra** – Lord of Island

**Dwipaada** – with two legs

**Dwirada** – elephant

**Dwijotamma** – best among Brahmins

**Dwivedi** – person who has knowledge of two Vedas

# E

**Eashana** – name of the heaven

**Ebhanan** – elephant faced Ganpati

**Eeksha** – looking

**Eepsu** – desire to have

**Eera** – wind

**Eeravati** – name of the river

**Eeraja** – name of Hanuman

**Eersha** – jealousy

**Eesh** – supreme, Lord Shiva

**Eeshana** – name of heaven

**Eeshtva** – superior

**Eeshvardatta** – given by God

**Eeshvara** – God

**Eeshwar** – God

**Eeshana** – the Sun

**Eil** – Sun of Earth

**Ekaagra** – concentration

**Ekaakshu** – a person with one eye

**Ekadanta** – the God with one tusk

**Ekaanta** – solitary

**Ekaatma** – alone

**Ekakundala** – Lord of the sea

**Ekalavya** – a Bheel boy famous for his devotion towards his teacher Dronacharya

**Ekalinga** – Lord Shiva

**Ekambera** – Lord Shiva, sky

**Ekama** – unit, digit

**Ekanga** – bodyguard

**Ekanatha** – famous king

**Ekata** – unity

**Ekath** – name of a famous Rishi
**Ekendra** – God
**Ekodar** – brother
**Ekrama** – honour

**Elesha** – king
**Eleyaraja** – king
**Eravantha** – son of Arjun and Uloopi
**Esha** – pleasure

# F

**Fanindra** – sheshnag, serpent

**Fannig** – lying on serpent (Vishnu)

**Fannish** – serpent, sheshnag

**Faiz** – gain

**Faiyaz** – artistic

**Fanishwara** – king of serpent

**Fanishwara Renu** – famous writter

**Fannibhushan** – Lord Shiva

**Fateh** – victory

**Fateh Chand** – conqueror of Moon

**Fateh Singh** – victor

**Fatik** – crystal

**Farhad** – happiness

**Farhat** – happiness

**Faraj** – equitable

**Farida** – wide

**Firdaus** – victory

**Firoze** – turquoise

# G

**Gaadhi** – father of Vishvamitra

**Gaadhaya** – Vishvamitra

**Gaalava** – the lordhra tree

**Gaayana** – singing

**Gabroo** – simple, young

**Gadaa** – a mace

**Gadaadhara** – the holder of mace

**Gadin** – Krishna

**Gadambera** – clouds

**Gagan** – sky

**Gaganchara** – moving in the sky

**Gagandhvaja** – the Sun

**Gagandipika** – the Sun

**Gaganaghosha** – thunder

**Gaganamani** – jewel of the sky

**Gaganaprakasha** – light of the sky

**Gaganasindhu** – Ganga

**Gaganaviharee** – one who moves in the sky

**Gahana** – who has the strength of an elephant

**Gaja** – an elephant

**Gajadanta** – an elephant's tusk

**Gajadhar** – one who can handle and elephant

**Gajakrishna** – name of a man

**Gajamukh** – Ganesh

**Gajanan** – Ganesh

**Gajananda** – Ganesh

**Gajapati** – Lord of the elephant

**Gajaratna** – pearl of Ganesha

**Gajaroopa** – Lord
Shiva

**Gajendra** – king of
the elephant

**Gamatee** – jolly,
happy

**Gambheera** –
serious, profound

**Gambheerasheela** –
serious character

**Gandhamadan** – a
large bea

**Gandharva** – a
singer

**Gandhara** – chief of
a group

**Gandharvasen** –
celestial musician

**Gangaditya** – a form
of the Sun

**Gangaputra** –
Bhishama

**Ganga Saagara** –
mouth of the
Ganges from where
it enters the sea

**Gangasuta** –
kartikeya, Bhisham

**Gangodaka** – water
of Ganges

**Ganikaa** – a
courtesan

**Garaldhara** – Lord
Shiva

**Garuda** – the bird of
Lord Vishnu

**Garudamaanikya** –
an emerald

**Gareeyasa** – very
precious

**Garudaketu** –
Vishnu, Krishna

**Garuditya** – Sun

**Garutmata** – a
heavenly bird

**Garva** – proud

**Gaunarda** – Rishi
Patanjali

**Gaurava** – Respect,
Proud

**Gauree Kant** – Lord
Shiva

**Gauree Shankara** –
Lord Shiva

**Gaureesha** –
Moonlight

**Gauranga** – fair complexioned, Lord Shiva

**Gautam** – name of Buddha

**Gavaaksha** – a bull eye

**Gavamrita** – cow-milk

**Gavendra** – Lord Vishnu

**Gaveshaka** – Research

**Gaveshnaa** – invention, discovery

**Gayan** – singing, sky

**Geet** – song

**Ghana** – cloud

**Ghanaaghana** – a thick cloud

**Ghanrasa** – camphor

**Ghansaara** – camphor

**Ghanshyama** – Lord Krishna

**Ghanvahana** – Lord Krishna

**Ghanaavalli** – creeper of cloud

**Ghantadhara** – wearing bell in the ear

**Ghata** – a pitcher

**Ghatja** – born from a pot

**Ghatasambhava** – Agastya

**Ghataudbhava** – born from a pot

**Ghorah** – Lord Shiva

**Ghosh** – noise

**Giri** – mountain

**Giridhara** – Lord Krishna

**Girijapati** – Lord Shiva

**Girikota** – the summit of mountain

**Girilala** – son of the mountain

**Girija Prasad** – blessing of Girija

**Girijanath** – Lord Shiva

**Girijaavallabha** – Lord Shiva

**Girindra** – the highest mountain

**Giripat** – Lord Shiva

**Giriraja** – himalaya

**Girisha** – Lord Shiva

**Girvaana** – language of the Gods

**Gobinda** – Lord Krishna

**Gokurna** – cows ear

**Gokula** – Herd of cows

**Gokulanatha** – Lord Krishna

**Gokulchanda** – Lord Krishna

**Gokulendra** – Lord Krishna

**Golakhnaath** – master of the Gokul

**Golokesha** – Lord Krishna

**Gomateshvara** – gem

**Gopal** – protector of cows

**Gopanandana** – son of cowherd

**Gopendra** – Lord Krishna

**Gopesha** – Lord Krishna

**Gopinaatha** – master of senses

**Goswami** – Lord of senses

**Gourishankara** – Lord Shiva

**Govinda** – Lord Krishna

**Govardhana** – a sacred mountain

**Grahadheesha** – the Sun

**Grahashraya** – polar star

**Grahesha** – Lord of the planets

**Granthika** – astrologer

**Gruheeta** – which is understood

**Gunaadhya** – rich in virtue and wisdom

**Gunadhara** – one who possess character

**Gunaratna** – jewel in virtue

**Gunaashrava** – excellent

**Gunjaka** – resonance

**Gunnidhi** – Lord Shiva

**Gunneshwara** – God

**Gurbachana** – the promise of teacher

**Gurdeepa** – light of the teacher

**Gurmeeta** – friend of the guru

# H

**Haafiz** – a religious person

**Hakikat Rai** – truthful

**Hansa** – swan, Sun, soul

**Hansaraj** – Lord Shiva, Sun

**Hamsa** – swan

**Hamid** – in praise of God

**Hanu** – cheek

**Hanumant** – a monkey chief

**Hanuman** – a monkey chief

**Haren** – Lord Shiva

**Harasidha** – eternal Shiva

**Hara** – Lord Shiva

**Hari** – Lord Vishnu

**Harbansa** – belonging to the family of Hari

**Harivansh** – belonging to the family of Lord

**Hari Charana** – at the feet of the Lord Vishnu

**Hari Chandana** – a kind of yellow paste of sandal

**Harihara** – Shiva and Vishnu together

**Hari Karana** – Hari and Karan

**Hari Krishna** – Lord Krishna

**Haridatta** – given by Hari

**Harideva** – Lord Krishna

**Harismita** – smile of Lord

**Harinanda** – Lord Krishna

**Harinaath** – whose Lord is Hari

**Hari vatsa** – name of Arjuna

**Harsha** – happiness, delight

**Harish** – Lord Krishna

**Harit** – Lord Vishnu

**Harshada** – giver of pleasure

**Harshak** – mountain

**Harshala** – a lover

**Harshula** – a deer

**Hasan** – generous, good looking

**Hasmukha** – smiling person

**Hastimall** – Lord Ganesha

**Hastin** – hand

**Hatakeshwara** – Lord of gold

**Havirdhaama** – place of sacrifice

**Heera** – diamond

**Heeraman** – diamond mind

**Helik** – the Sun

**Hemachandra** – golden Moon

**Hemadri** – golden Moon

**Hemal** – a musical note

**Hemkar** – Lord Shiva

**Hemkesh** – Lord Shiva

**Hemkanti** – having lustre of gold

**Hemang** – with limbs of gold

**Hemanka** – adorn with gold

**Hemanta** – winter

**Hemantanath** – Lord of winter season

**Hempushpa** – jasmine

**Hemshaila** – a mountain

**Hemshankha** – Lord Vishnu

**Hemendu** – golden Moon

**Hemendra** – Lord of gold

**Hemanga** – one having a shining body
**Hamavatinandana** – son of hemavati
**Hemvat** – the snowy mountain
**Heramba** – boastful, Ganesha
**Hima** – snow
**Himabhanu** – Moon
**Himachala** – himalaya
**Himdhara** – himalaya
**Himadari** – himalaya
**Himalaya** – abode of snow
**Himakiran** – Moon
**Himanshu** – the Moon
**Himashala** – unmoving
**Himmat Singh** – courageous
**Himval** – pearl
**Hira** – diamond
**Hiranmaya** – golden
**Hiranya** – wealth

**Hiranyada** – giver of wealth
**Hiranyaksha** – one having golden eyes
**Hirendra** – Lord of diamond
**Hiresha** – kind of gem
**Hitesha** – good for others
**Hridanshu** – the Moon
**Hridaya** – heart
**Hridyesha** – a beloved person
**Hridyeshawara** – husband
**Hridyanath** – beloved
**Hridyarama** – with Rama in the heart
**Hridyanand** – heart full of joy
**Hrishikesha** – Lord Vishnu
**Hrishikeshwara** – Lord Krishna
**Hrisheeka** – Lord Krishna

# I

**Ibhanana** – face of an elephant

**Ibhapaala** – protector of elephant

**Idaa** – speech, the Earth

**Ikshu** – eyelash

**Ikshvaaku** – name of the king of solar dynasty

**Ikhtiar** – right, trust

**Iloosha** – name of man

**Indiralaya** – the blue lotus

**Indivara** – blue lotus. fully blossomed

**Indiresh** – Lord Indra

**Indra** – Raingod

**Indrabha** – light of the rain god

**Indraditya** – Sun and Indra

**Indradatta** – Lord Indra, the giver

**Indradyumna** – splendour of Indra

**Indragiri** – mountain

**Indragopa** – Indra as protector

**Indraghosh** – voice of Indra

**Indrajaa** – decendent of Indra

**Indrajit** – one who has conquered Lord Indra

**Indranila** – emareld

**Indrapal** – protected by Indra

**Indraverman** – name of a warrior

**Indravadan** – like Indra's face

**Indubhushan** – the Moon

**Indudhar** – the sky

**Indukanth** – the Moon

**Indukesri** – Moon lion

**Indukireet** – Lord Shiva

**Indulal** – Moon's lustre

**Induratna** – pearl

**Indushekhara** – planet mercury

**Inesha** – king of kings

**Iresha** – Lord of the Earth

**Irmaa** – the Sun

**Ishita** – mastery

**Ish** – God

**Isha** – ruler

**Ishma** – God of love the spring

**Isar** – Lord Shiva

**Ishita** – beloved

**Ishtadeva** – favourite God

**Ishwara** – God

**Ishwaraprasada** – with grace of God

# J

**Jagabandhana** – worshipped by all

**Jagachaksha** – the supreme being

**Jagaadhara** – support of the universe

**Jagadeva** – Lord of the universe

**Jagadeesha** – Lord of the universe

**Jagadeeshawara** – Lord of the universe

**Jagadnanda** – joy of the universe

**Jagajeeta** – conqueror of the universe

**Jagajivana** – life of the universe

**Jagesha** – master of the universe

**Jagmohan** – Lord Krishna

**Jagnarayana** – the Lord of universe

**Jagannatha** – the Lord of universe

**Jagannidhi** – Lord Vishnu

**Jagata** – universe, world

**Jagataprakasha** – light of the universe

**Jai or Jay** – victory

**Jaichanda** – victory of the Moon

**Jaidayala** – victory of the kindness

**Jaideva** – victory of God

**Jaidratha** – name of a king of Mahabharata

**Jaigopala** – victory of Lord Krishna

**Jaipaula** – victory of Lord Brahma

**Jaishankara** – victory of Lord Shiva

**Jaishree** – honour of victory

**Jaisukha** – success

**Jaisudha** – nectar of victory

**Jayanta** – Lord Vishnu

**Jayatsena** – Nakula during exile

**Jalada** – cloud

**Jaladhara** – cloud

**Jalaadhi** – sea

**Jalaj** – lotus

**Jalala** – glory

**Jalarka** – reflection of Sun in water

**Jalaavaran** – rainy season

**Jalendra** – Lord Shiva

**Jaleshwara** – ocean

**Jamnadasa** – servant of Yamuna

**Janaardhana** – helpful to people

**Janak** – father of Sita

**Janadeva** – the king

**Janadhinatha** – Lord Vishnu

**Janamadhipa** – Lord Shiva

**Janamitra** – friend of people

**Janamejaya** – son of Parikshita

**Janendra** – the king

**Janesha** – the king

**Jaspal** – Lord of the universe

**Jaswant** – victorious

**Jataa** – twisted hair

**Jataadhar** – Lord Shiva

**Jataatanka** – Lord Shiva

**Jataayu** – king of the vulture

**Jati** – twisted hair

**Jatin** – Lord Shiva

**Jugala** – pair

**Jawahara** – jewel

**Jawala** – fire

**Jawala Prasada** – gift from fire

**Jawalanta** – shining
**Jayin** – being victorous
**Jayaditya** – victory of Sun
**Jayakaanta** – pleasing
**Jayashekhara** – victory
**Jeeva** – crest
**Jeevan** – life
**Jeevesh** – the God
**Jeevraja** – Lord of life
**Jevaini** – a sage who is known for his philosophy
**Jhanshankar** – one who can control himself
**Jigisha** – want to conquer
**Jignyassu** – thirsty for knowledge
**Jina** – victory
**Jinanandana** – victory of happiness

**Jinavimala** – famous author
**Jinendra** – Lord of life, Lord of victory, a winner of desires
**Jinesha** – name of an Arhata
**Jineshawara** – name of an Arhata
**Jinodaya** – jain Suri
**Jishnu** – triumphant
**Jitavrata** – one who keeps his promise
**Jivaraja** – Lord of life
**Jnaan** – knowledge
**Jnaandeepa** – light of knowledge
**Jnaandeva** – God of knowledge
**Jnaananagni** – knowledge of fire
**Jnnanprabha** – shining with knowledge
**Jnaanprakasha** – light of knowledge

**Jnaaneshwara** – a wise person

**Joginder** – a high class Yogi

**Jograja** – Lord Krishna

**Jorawar Singh** – a powerful, brave person

**Jyoti Dhara** – holder of flame

**Jyoti Prakash** – light of the flame

**Jyotiranjana** – joyous flame

**Jyestha** – pre-eminent, elder

**Jyotsnesha** – Lord of Moonlight

# K

**Kaakutshtha** – a sovereign

**Kaalanjaya** – conqueror of time

**Kaalidaasa** – slave of Goddess Kaali

**Kaalindi** – river Yamuna

**Kaalindi Krishna** – the elder brother of Lord Krishna

**Kaamaballabha** – the Moonlight

**Kaamadeva** – the Lord of love

**Kaamamaalina** – Lord Ganesha

**Kaamashakh** – the season of spring

**Kaamjaa** – born of desire

**Kaamran** – success

**Kaanhaa** – Lord Krishna

**Kaapaalin** – Lord Shiva

**Kaarandava** – a variety of duck

**Kaarti** – month of Kartik

**Kaartika** – belongs to the month of Kartik

**Kaashi** – grass

**Kaatyaayana** – a sage

**Kabeera** – name of a famous poet

**Kadamba** – name of a tree

**Kaikeya** – a king of Kekayas

**Kailaash** – abode of Lord Shiva

**Kailaash Chandra** – Lord Shiva

**Kairva** – white Lotus

**Kaishika** – with beautiful hair

**Kaivalya** – final attainment or emanicipation

**Kaivarta** – a fisherman

**Kajjala** – applied to eyes or eyelashes

**Kakanda** – gold

**Kakudmi** – mountain

**Kalaanidhi** – the Moon, treasure of arts

**Kalaapee** – peacock

**Kalankash** – lion

**Kalendu** – Moon

**Kalinda** – the Sun

**Kalinga** – an ancient city

**Kalpa** – determination

**Kalpaka** – rite

**Kalpataru** – the tree of paradise

**Kalyaana** – happy, blessed

**Kalyaanama** – blessed

**Kamal** – lotus

**Kamalakaant** – the Sun

**Kamalesha** – Lord Vishnu

**Kamashwara** – Lord of love

**Kamboja** – shell

**Kamlaakara** – a lake full of lotus

**Kamlaakara** – lotus handed

**Kanaka** – gold

**Kanakva** – small kite

**Kanchan** – gold

**Kandarpa** – Lord of love, Kamdeva

**Kandarpa** – the God of love, Kamdeva

**Kandot** – white lotus

**Kaneera** – kaner tree

**Kanhaiyaa** – Lord Krishna

**Kanishka** – little, name of the king of Kushaana dynasty

**Kanja** – lotus

**Kanjaara** – peacock

**Kanjana** – Lord of love

**Kanka** – crane

**Kansa** – goblet

**Kansaarti** – Lord Krishna

**Kansari** – Lord Krishna

**Kanu** – Lord Krishna

**Kanva** – name of the Rishi who was father of Shakuntala

**Kanwar** – prince

**Kapaali** – Lord Shiva

**Kapaatapaani** – Lord Shiva

**Kapeendra** – king of monkey Sugriva

**Kapindra** – Lord Shiva

**Kapinjala** – partridge

**Kapish** – reddish brown

**Kapoora** – camphor

**Karamashrestha** – greatest in action

**Karana** – a famous warrior and son of Kunti

**Karandeva** – wind

**Karanjeet** – conqueror of Karna

**Karnandu** – ear ring

**Karnkaa** – ear ring

**Kartaara** – creator

**Kartikeya** – son of Lord Shiva

**Karun** – compassion

**Karunaakara** – full of pity

**Karunanidhi** – full of compassion

**Karveeraya** – a brave peres

**Karvinda** – name of famous writer

**Karvira** – a cow of good variety

**Kashaaku** – the Sun

**Kashmeeraa** – a person belonging to Kashmir

**Kashyap** – tortoise

**Kashyapa** – Garuda

{47}

**Kasturee** – musk
**Kataka** – bracelet
**Kathaa** – story
**Kathaarnava** – stories about sea
**Kathaka** – story narrator
**Kaumaara** – youthful
**Kaunteya** – son of Kunti
**Kausha** – silken
**Kaushika** – Lord Indra, Vishwamitra
**Kaustubha** – precious stone
**Kautilya** – master of diplomacy
**Kavana** – water
**Kavasha** – a sage
**Kavel** – lotus
**Kavendu** – poet Balmiki
**Kavi** – poet
**Kaviraaya** – best poet
**Kedaar** – Lord Shiva

**Kedarnaatha** – Lord Shiva
**Keertivardhana** – increasing fame
**Kesara** – saffron
**Kesari Kishore** – young man
**Keshava** – possessing fine and lustrous hair, Lord Vishnu
**Keshika** – having lustrous hair
**Keshin** – lion
**Ketan** – flag
**Ketan** – a house
**Keval** – only
**Kevala Kishore** – absolutely young
**Keyura** – an armlet
**Khaabhiraama** – Lord Shiva
**Khachita** – fastening
**Khadim** – servant
**Khadir** – Lord Indra
**Khaga** – bird
**Khagendra** – king of birds

**Khagesha** – Lord of birds, Garuda

**Khageshwara** – eagle, Garuda

**Khajit** – conquering heaven

**Khakuntala** – Lord Shiva

**Khamani** – the Sun

**Khandra** – part

**Khandana** – breaking

**Khandaparashu** – parshuraama

**Khanjana** – sword

**Kharaanshu** – the Moon

**Khazaana** – treasure

**Khechra** – a bird

**Khilaavana** – the Sun

**Khokhuna** – a boy

**Khushamana** – happy mind

**Khushilaa** – happy man

**Khushvanta** – joyous person

**Kim** – bird

**Kinjalka** – blossoming of the flower

**Kinkira** – Lord of love

**Kinnara** – demi-god

**Kiraat** – hunter

**Kiranmaya** – radiant

**Kireeta** – crest

**Kiritt** – the crown

**Kishalaya** – a sprout

**Kishore** – young

**Kohinoor** – mountain of light, name of a diamond

**Kokila** – cuckoo

**Komal** – soft

**Koojamohan** – the God of war

**Kovida** – learned man

**Kratu** – power

**Kripa** – the brother of Kripi

**Kripaashankara** – Lord Shiva, kindness of Lord Shiva

**Krishanakant** – beloved of Krishna

**Krishna** – dark blue

**Krishna Kishore** – young Krishna

**Krishnachaarya** – Krishna as a teacher

**Kshaapaakar** – the Moon

**Kshamaapati** – king

**Kshapaanaatha** – Lord of the night

**Ksheera** – milk

**Ksheetishwara** – the Lord of the Earth

**Kshemendra** – a laureat

**Kshetrapaala** – protector of the Earth

**Kshitija** – horizon

**Kshitinaatha** – a sovereign

**Kshitindra** – king

**Kshitipaala** – protector of the Earth

**Kshitisha** – Lord of the world

**Kubera** – Lord of treasures

**Kulbhushana** – jewel of family

**Kuldeepa** – lighted lamp of the family

**Kuleen** – of noble birth

**Kulika** – from the noble family

**Kulwant** – from a noble family

**Kumaara** – prince

**Kumaaraswaami** – name of a poet

**Kumaaravaahana** – a peacock

**Kumaarila** – a famous teacher

**Kumbhaja** – Rishi Agastya

**Kumbhakarna** – brother of Raavana

**Kumudanaatha** – Lord of lilies

**Kunaala** – son of king Ashoka
**Kundala** – ear ring
**Kundana** – gold
**Kunja** – a grove
**Kunjabehaaree** – Lord Krishna
**Kunjara** – an elephant
**Kuntala** – a lock of hair
**Kuntesha** – master of spears
**Kuntibhoja** – name of a king who adopted Kunti
**Kuranga** – a deer
**Kurma** – tortoise
**Kuru** – an ancient city

**Kush** – son of Lord Rama
**Kushaadaa** – straight forward
**Kushaada** – sharp mind
**Kushal** – skilled, clever
**Kushilava** – singer
**Kusumaakar** – season of spring
**Kusumachandra** – saffron
**Kusumbha** – saffron
**Kusumit** – bouquet of flowers
**Karakishalaya** – a soft and tender hand

# L

**Laabha** – profit
**Laalamani** – ruby
**Laalitya** – desire
**Laasya** – a name of a dance
**Lagana** – auspicious time
**Lajpatrai** – one who keeps dignity
**Lakhan** – short form of Lakshman
**Lakshana** – special qualities
**Lakshapati** – a millionaire
**Lakshmana** – fortunate, younger brother of Lord Rama
**Lakshmidhara** – bearer of Lakshmi
**Lakshmikaanta** – belover of Lakshmi

**Lakshminarayan** – Lakshmi and Narayan
**Lakshya** – the aim
**Lalit** – charming
**Lalitaadity** – beautiful Sun
**Lalitamohana** – attractive and beautiful
**Lambodar** – Lord Ganesha
**Lankesha** – Lord of Lanka
**Latakara** – a mass of creepers
**Latif** – elegant
**Lavanaa** – lusture
**Lavaraaja** – son of Lord Rama
**Laxmiramana** – Lord Vishnu
**Leelaadhara** – Lord Vishnu

**Lekhraaja** – king of writing

**Lochna** – eyes

**Lohita** – handsome

**Lokaanand** – joy of the world

**Lokamaheshwara** – Lord Krishna

**Lokanaatha** – Lord of the world

**Lokanaayaka** – leader of the world

**Lokaprakaasha** – light of the world

**Lokesha** – Lord of the world

**Lokeshwara** – Lord of the world

**Lomaharshna** – one who thrills

**Lomasa** – hairy

**Lubdhaka** – a hunter

# M

**Maadhava** – Lord Vishnu

**Maanasa** – the mind

**Maanavendra** – king among the men

**Maanika** – ruby

**Maaniky** – jewel

**Maardava** – softness

**Maartanda** – Sun

**Maaruti** – Lord Hanumaana

**Maatanga** – an elephant

**Maatarishvan** – the wind

**Madan** – Lord Krishna

**Madana** – toxic

**Madhughosha** – sweet sound

**Madhukara** – honey

**Madhupa** – a person who drinks honey

**Madhura** – sweet

**Madhusudana** – Lord Krishna, destroyer of evil

**Magana** – egrossed

**Maghvana** – Lord Indra

**Mahaabali** – very strong

**Mahaananda** – blissfully happy

**Mahaarishi** – great sage

**Mahabali** – with prowess

**Mahaishi** – wise

**Mahanidhi** – large treasure

**Mahaaveera** – very brave, twenty fourth tirthankar of Jains

**Maheenaatha** – Lord of the Earth

**Maheepaala** – protector of the Earth

**Mahesha** – Lord Shiva

**Maheshawara** – Lord Shiva

**Mahidev** – Brahman

**Mahin** – kingly

**Mahindra** – Lord Indra

**Mahipal** – the king

**Mahish** – the king

**Mahtab** – the Moon

**Mainaaka** – son of himalaya

**Maitreya** – friend

**Makaradhavja** – crocodile bannered

**Makrand** – honey bee

**Malaya** – celestial garden of Indra

**Mallanaaga** – name of Vaatsyaayana, the author of Kaamasutra

**Manana** – meditation

**Manaranjana** – delighting the mind

**Manas** – mind

**Manasakaanta** – one who pleases mind

**Manasija** – the God of love

**Manasukha** – joy of the mind

**Manava** – man

**Manbhirama** - posessor of happy mind

**Mandaara** – flower

**Mandana** – cheerful, ornament

**Mandaraa** – coral tree

**Manendra** – king of the mind

**Mangla** – holy blessing

**Manglesha** – Lord Vishnu

**Mani** – a diamond

**Manidhara** – one who wears jewels

**Manigreeva** – neck of jewel

**Manika** – jewel

**Manikarana** -- jewel of ear

**Manindra** – diamond

**Manishankara** – Lord Shiva

**Manishi** – learned

**Manjeeta** – the conqueror of mind

**Manmatha** – Kaamdeva

**Mamathabandhu** – Moon

**Manobhaava** – the emotions which exist in the mind

**Manobhava** – imaginary

**Manohara** – one who charms the mind

**Manoja** – born of the mind

**Manojna** – attractive

**Manojya** – pleasing to mind

**Manoranjana** – one which makes the mind happy, entertainment

**Manoratha** – desire

**Manotosha** – satisfaction

**Manu** – name of an ancient philosopher

**Manuja** – born of Manu

**Manyu** – mind

**Manyudeva** – God of spirit

**Maraala** – swan

**Mareechi** – ray of light

**Markandeya** – writer of Puranas

**Martand** – the Sun

**Marut** – breeze

**Marutpati** – Lord of the wind

**Mathuradaasa** – the servant of Mathura

**Mathuresha** – Lord of Mathura

**Matsyandra** – king of the fishes

**Mauli** – foremost

**Maulika** – original

**Maulina** – best

**Mayanka** – the Moon
**Mayukha** – peacock
**Mayura** – peacock
**Medhavin** – a learned man
**Megha** – cloud
**Meghabhuti** – lightening
**Meghadoota** – cloud as a messenger
**Meghavarna** – as dark as cloud
**Mehula** – rain
**Merutunga** – jain Muni
**Mihir** – the Sun
**Mihir Kiran** – ray of Sun
**Mihira** – an ancient astrologer
**Milinda** – a bee
**Mitesha** – a person who have few desires
**Mithilesha** – king Janaka, the king of Mithila
**Mithun** – zodiac sign

**Mithuna** – couple
**Mitryu** – having a friendly mind
**Mitula** – limited
**Modakvallabha** – Lord Ganesha
**Mohaka** – fragrance, a person who attracts
**Mohana** – charming
**Mohita** – charming one who attracts others
**Moorthy** – statue
**Moti** – pearl
**Mrigank** – Moon
**Mrigmada** – musk
**Mritunjaya** – one who attains victory over death
**Mrudu** – Lord Shiva
**Mrudula** – softy and sweetly spoken
**Mrugaksha** – deer eyed
**Mrugendra** – king of animals

**Mrugesha** – Lord of animals

**Mudagala** – name of the sage

**Mudita** – happy

**Mukhendu** – face like Moon

**Muktesha** – Lord of free person

**Mukula** – bud

**Mukulita** – fully blossomed

**Mukuta** – crown

**Mularaaja** – king of roots

**Mulkaraaja** – king of the country

**Muneeshwara** – Lord of the munis

**Munindra** – Lord Indra

**Murajit** – victory over mura demon

**Murari** – Lord Krishna

# N

**Nakula** – a mongoose
**Naaga** – snake
**Naagaarjuna** – an ancient buddhist teacher
**Naagadhar** – Lord Shiva
**Naagandra** – chief of the serpent
**Naagchuda** – serpent crested
**Naagesha** – serpent prince
**Naageshawara** – name of a prince
**Naamadeva** – Lord Vishnu
**Naamdhaari** – in the name only
**Naanaka** – griefless, first guru of the Sikhs
**Naarayana** – Lord Vishnu
**Naarada** – a celebrated Rishi
**Naayaka** – actor
**Nabhaketana** – the Sun
**Nabhkanti** – splendour of the skies
**Nabhomani** – sky jewel
**Nachiketa** – a sage
**Nachiketa** – fire
**Naga** – steady
**Nagaja** – born of the mountains
**Nagendra** – Lord of mountains
**Nagesha** – the king of mountain Himalaya
**Nahusha** – father of yayaati
**Naishadha** – a king of the Nishadas
**Nakshatra** – stars

**Nala** – a kind of reed, a famous king

**Nalina** – lotus

**Nalinaaksha** – lotus eyed

**Nanda** – delighted

**Nandakishore** – Lord Krishna

**Nandana** – a son

**Nandavardhan** – increaser of happiness

**Nandighosh** – cry of joy

**Nandika** – pleasure

**Nandikesha** – Lord Shiva

**Nandikeshvara** – Lord Shiva

**Naraadhipa** – Lord of the people

**Naranaarraayana** – Lord Krishna

**Narendra** – God

**Naresha** – king

**Nareshvara** – Lord of the people

**Narottama** – best among the man

**Narvar** – best person

**Narveera** – brave person

**Nata** – actor, a juggler

**Natvara** – Lord Krishna

**Naval** – fresh

**Navaneeta** – soft, new

**Navanidhiana** – possessing nine different treasures

**Navaratna** – precious jewels

**Naveena** – new, young

**Navendu** – new Moon

**Navyakriti** – Lord Krishna

**Nayana** – eyes

**Nayanasukeha** – pleasure of seeing

**Neelaambara** – dressed in blue clothes

**Neelagriva** – Lord Shiva

**Neelkantha** – Lord Shiva, peacock

**Neelambaja** – blue lotus

**Neerada** – water giver, cloud

**Neeraja** – water born

**Neerava** – peaceful, without any sound or life

**Neeteepa** – protector of the law

**Neetisha** – well versed in law

**Nehaal** – happy

**Nelesha** – Lord Krishna

**Netrapaala** – protector of eyes

**Niauppama** – matchless

**Nidhisha** – Lord of treasure

**Nighna** – dependent

**Nihaara** – fog

**Niketa** – residence

**Niketana** – residence

**Nikhat** – fragrance

**Nikhila** – entire

**Nikhilesha** – the Lord of entire universe

**Nikumbha** – son of the Prahalada

**Nilaya** – heaven

**Ninaada** – sound

**Nipuna** – expert

**Niraja** – without passion

**Niranjana** – truthful, spotless, Lord Shiva

**Nirbhaya** – fearless

**Nirmala** – pure

**Nirmalundu** – clear Moon

**Nirvaana** – attainment

**Nirvaira** – without enmity

**Nischala** – without movement

**Nischinta** – without any anxiety

**Nishaadhisha** – the Moon

**Nishaanta** – end of night, calm
**Nishaatha** – polished
**Nishitapati** – Moon
**Nishika** – ornament
**Nishkaama** – without any work or desire
**Nishoka** – happy
**Nissima** – unbound
**Nitina** – Lord of right path
**Nitya** – everyday
**Nityaananda** – ever happy

**Nivedana** – request
**Nivedita** – offer of God
**Nivruti** – one who is separated from the world
**Nrideva** – God of men
**Nridharman** – Lord Krishna
**Nrikesari** – man lion
**Nrimna** – strength
**Nripa** – king
**Nrupendra** – king of kings

# O

**Occhav** – festive occasion

**Ogaan** – wave

**Ogha** – rapid flow of water

**Oja** – bright

**Ojas** – strength of body

**Ojaspati** – a name of Buddha

**Ojasvi** – possessing power and strength

**Oka** – a house

**Om** – affirmation

**Omananda** – delight of OM

**Omjaa** – born of OM

**Omkaar** – the sacred mantra

**Omkaarnath** – Lord Vishnu

**Omprakash** – light of OM

**Omrao** – king

**Omswaroopa** – manifestation of OM

**Oomjam** – enthusiasm

**Oordhva** – towards the sky

**Oorjita** – powerful

**Oormila** – emotional

**Ordradeshna** – name of Orissa

**Orgharatha** – name of the son of oghavat

**Oudichya** – northern

# P

**Paanini** – name of an ancient grammarian

**Paraashara** – an ancient Rishi

**Paarus** – touchstone which turns metal into gold

**Paarindra** – lion

**Paaritosha** – satisfaction, prize

**Paarshada** – friend

**Paartha** – Arjuna

**Paarthav** – greatness

**Paavaka** – fire

**Paavan** – pure, pious

**Padamaksha** – lotus eyed

**Padamaapati** – Lord Vishnu

**Padamnabha** – lotus

**Padmadhisha** – Lord Vishnu

**Padmakara** – lotus pond

**Padmin** – elephant, lotus

**Palaka** – eyelashes

**Pallaba** – new leaves

**Panchabaana** – five arrows

**Panchanana** – Lord Shiva

**Pankaja** – lotus

**Pannaalaala** – emerald

**Paraaga** – pollen

**Paraanjaya** – Lord of sea

**Paraashara** – a name of ancient sage

**Param** – the best, top

**Paramaatmana** – God

**Paramahansa** – supreme being

**Parangada** – Lord Shiva

**Paranjaya** – conqueror

**Paranjaya** – varuna

**Parantapa** – a hero

**Paresha** – supreme God

**Paridhanaa** – clothes

**Parijaata** – celestial flower

**Pariketa** – against desire

**Parikshita** – a name of ancient sage

**Parimala** – fragrance

**Parimil** – fragrance of sandal

**Parajanya** – rain

**Parmesha** – Lord Shiva

**Parmeshshwara** – God

**Parnal** – with lots of leaves

**Parshurama** – an ancient sage

**Parvata** – mountain

**Pashupati** – Lord Shiva

**Pataanjali** – name of a yoga teacher

**Pataasha** – a flowering tree

**Pataasharanjana** – as beautiful as Pataasha

**Patanjali** – an ancient author

**Pathika** – traveller

**Pavana** – air, breeze

**Payoda** – cloud

**Phaindra** – the celestial snake

**Pingesha** – Agni Deva

**Pitaambera** – Lord Krishna

**Piungalaksha** – a person with brown eyes

**Piyusha** – nectar

**Poojay** – worshiped

**Poojit** – worshiped

**Pooran** – complete

**Poornaananda** – joy of accomplishment

**Poornaayu** – complete life

**Poornaya** – complete

**Poorvasha** – Lord of the east

**Pooshan** – a person who nourishes

**Praalambha** – to take hold of

**Praan** – life

**Prabala** – coral intensity

**Prabhaagachandra** – part of the Moon

**Prabhaakara** – Sun

**Prabhaank** – symbol of light

**Prabhaas** – lustrous

**Prabhaash** – one who knows many words, well versed in language

**Prabhaat** – morning

**Prabhaav** – effect

**Prabhagachandra** – part of the Moon

**Prabodha** – good advice

**Prabodhan** – knowledge

**Prabuddha** – intelligent a sage

**Prachura** – abundant

**Pradeep** – lamp

**Pradosha** – dusk

**Pradyot** – very bright

**Pradyumna** – mighty

**Prafulla** – blooming

**Pragnyakara** – very intelligent

**Prahlaada** – joy, son of Hrinyakashyap

**Prajana** – wise, intelligent

**Prajeet** – victorous

**Prajesha** – Lord of people, Lord Brahma

**Prajita** – kind

**Prajnaa** – wise

**Prajnesha** – Lord of wisdom

**Prajyaana** – intelligent
**Prakaash** – light
**Prakaashaaditya** – the shining Sun
**Prakat** – natural manifested
**Pralaya** – disaster, himalaya
**Pramati** – intelligent
**Pramda** – delighted
**Pramod** – joyous
**Pramodan** – joyous
**Pranava** – young, syllable OM
**Pranaya** – love marriage
**Pranetaa** – leader
**Prani** – modest
**Pranita** – modest
**Pranjala** – complicated
**Pranjeevana** – life
**Prasanna** – happy
**Prasbodhan** – knowledge
**Prasoona** – blossom
**Prataapa** – fame

**Prateeka** – sign, symbol, first word of the sentence
**Prateera** – bank of the river
**Prateeta** – manifested
**Pratosha** – very happy
**Pratula** – plenty
**Praval** – extremely fierce
**Pravara** – a stream, chief
**Praveena** – expert
**Praveera** – brave
**Prayaaga** – a holy city where three rivers confluence
**Preetisha** – Lord of love
**Premaananda** – joy of love
**Premanidhi** – ocean of love
**Premasaagara** – ocean of love
**Premendu** – Moon love

**Pritam** – lover
**Prithu** – spacious
**Pritjviraaja** – king of the Earth
**Priyaanshu** – well dressed
**Priyanka** – kadamb tree
**Priyankara** – lover
**Priyaranjana** – lover
**Pratipaal** – defender
**Pukhraaj** – yellow stone
**Pulakesin** – a king in ancient times
**Pulisha** – a sage
**Pulkesha** – joyous

**Pundaalika** – lotus
**Puneeta** – pure
**Purandu** – full Moon
**Purshottama** – Lord Vishnu
**Puru** – an ancient king
**Purujeeta** – victory over the city
**Pushaan** – the Sun
**Pushkara** – blue lotus
**Pushpendra** – king among flower
**Pushpendu** – white lotus
**Pushpesha** – Lord of flower

**Qamar** – Full Moon
**Qasim** – old
  generation

**Qutub** – tall,
  of books

# R

**Raadh** – favour
**Raaja** – king
**Raajaamsaa** – flamingo
**Raajakumara** – prince
**Raajarishi** – Lord of Rishis
**Raajavilochana** – a person with beautiful eyes
**Raajeeva** – lotus
**Raajevalochana** – Lord Vishnu
**Raajyavardhana** – one who makes the kingdom prosper
**Raakesha** – Lord of the night
**Raakhaala** – to save
**Raama Kumara** – youth
**Raamaprasad** – blessing of Rama
**Raamila** – lover
**Raamveera** – hero of the battle
**Raavana** – demon king of Sri Lanka
**Rachita** – created
**Raghava** – Lord Rama
**Raghu** – family of Lord Rama
**Raghunaath** – Lord Rama
**Raghunandan** – Lord Rama
**Raghupati** – Lord Rama
**Raghuveera** – Lord Rama
**Raghvendra** – Lord Rama
**Rahasya** – secret
**Rahmaana** – merciful

**Rahul** – son of Lord Buddha

**Raj** – kingdom

**Rajan** – king

**Rajas** – mastery

**Rajat** – silver

**Rajat Shubhra** – as white as silver

**Rajatamaabha** – name of the man

**Rajendra** – king

**Rajesha** – king

**Rajita** – decorated

**Rajneesha** – Moon

**Rajnikaant** – Lord of night

**Raktabeeja** – name of the demon

**Rama** – Lord Rama

**Ramachhoda** – a person who leaves the field

**Raman** – pleasing

**Ramanimohana** – one who attracts a beautiful woman

**Ramanuja** – a great mathematician and astrologer

**Ramapati** – Lord Vishnu

**Ramesh** – Lord Vishnu

**Rameshwara** – Lord Rama, Lord Shiva

**Ramineeka** – handsome

**Ramita** – omnipresent

**Ramjani** – a person who is born in the month of Ramzan

**Rana** – war

**Ranehsa** – Lord Shiva

**Rangabehri** – one who plays with colours

**Ranjana** – pleasure

**Ranjeeta** – one who wins battles

**Raochana** – red Lotus

**Rahesha** – Lord of taste

**Rashanaa** – woman's girdle

**Rashid** – who guides to correct path

**Rashmi** – rays of the Sun

**Rashmikaanta** – Lord of the rays

**Rashmikety** – one who has a banner of rays

**Rashmimohana** – one who is delighted in the morning Sun rays

**Rasika** – a person who appreciates the beauty

**Rasikeshewara** – Lord Krishna

**Rateesha** – Kaamdeva

**Rathpati** – Lord of chariot

**Rathin** – receiving Warrior

**Ratidndra** – warrior

**Ratideva** – Kamdeva

**Ratiguna** – name of Gandharva

**Ratiramana** – God of love

**Ratiramaa** – kaamdeva

**Ratna** – precious stones

**Ratnaakara** –mine of jewels

**Ratnaayaka** – ruby

**Ratnadhipati** – Kubera

**Ratnagarbh** – Kubera

**Ratnagiri** – name of a mountain

**Ratnakirti** – Lord Buddha

**Ratnakoota** – name of a mountain

**Ratnam** – precious stone

**Ratneesh** – Kubera

**Ratneshwara** – Lord of the jewel

**Ravi** – Sun

**Ravija** – born of the Sun

**Ravikaanta** – rays of the Sun

**Ravikar** – rays of the Sun

**Ravikeerti** – one whose fame is like Sun

**Ravikula** – the family of the Sun

**Ravinaatha** – lotus

**Ravindra** – the Sun

**Raviranjana** – as dazzling as Sun

**Ravisha** – as dazzling as Sun

**Ripumalla** – name of a king

**Ripusudan** – shatrughana, destroyer of enemy

**Rishabha** – morality

**Rishabhadeva** – Lord of morality

**Risheeka** – Lord Shiva

**Rituraaja** – spring

**Rochisha** – brightness

**Rohita** – red colour

**Roopaka** – features

**Radheya** – Karna

**Ruchira** – sweet

**Rudradeva** – Lord Shiva

**Rukma** – gold

**Rupam** – beauty

**Rupin** – beautiful body

# S

**Saagara** – sea
**Saajana** – beloved
**Saaketa** – Ayodhyaa
**Saaketa** – Lord Krishna
**Saamanta** – the chief of a district
**Saanand** – having joy together
**Saandeepni** – name of a sage who was teacher of Lord Krishna
**Saaranga** – spotted deer, the peacock
**Saatyaki** – a warrior of Mahabharata
**Sabindu** – a mountain
**Sacchidaananda** – full of bliss
**Sachina** – Lord Indra
**Sachipati** – Lord Indra

**Sachirt** – consciousness
**Sadananda** – eternally blissed, Lord Shiva
**Sagun** – possessor of good qualities
**Sahatra** – one thousand
**Sahdeva** – the companion of the God
**Sahila** – the bank of the river
**Sai** – God, Lord
**Sainath** – God of gods
**Sajal** – moist
**Sajjana** – gentleman
**Saklendu** – full Moon
**Samara** – battle
**Samarendu** – Lord Vishnu
**Samartha** – efficient, powerful

**Samasta** – the universe

**Samaveda** – one of the four Veda

**Samaya** – time

**Sambhava** – possible

**Sameecha** – the ocean

**Sameera** – breeze

**Samichi** – going right

**Samidhaa** – an offering to the sacred fire

**Sampata** – Lord Vishnu

**Samundra** – sea

**Samvatasra** – year

**Sanchaya** – collection

**Sandeepana** – a sage

**Sandeepta** – excited

**Sangati** – companion

**Sangeeta** – music

**Sangrama** – battle

**Sanjaya** – the victory

**Sanjeev** – the life

**Sankalpa** – resolved

**Sanketa** – signal

**Sannidhi** – proximity

**Sansaar** – the world

**Santosha** – contentment

**Sanyoga** – combination

**Sanyukta** – united

**Sapana** – dream

**Saptashava** – the Sun

**Saral** – easy, simple

**Sareshavara** – Lord

**Sarjita** – one who wins the war

**Sarvada** – Lord Shiva

**Sarvakaama** – Lord Shiva

**Sarvottma** – the best

**Satyajit** – true to victory

**Satyaakaama** – truthlover

**Satyendra** – a person who is always truthful

**Sauparn** – a Vedic Mantra

**Saushthava** – good expression

**Shaavaka** – child

**Shabdhprakash** – glory of the words

**Shaguna** – auspicious

**Shaila** – Lord Shiva, mountain

**Shailendra** – Lord Shiva

**Shailendra** – the mountain

**Shaileshwara** – Lord Shiva

**Shakra** – powerful

**Shakti** – strength

**Shaktivallabha** – lover of Shakti

**Shakuna** – good omen

**Shakuni** – a bird, a famous character in Mahabharata

**Shalena** – modest

**Shambhu** – Lord Shiva

**Shankar** – Lord Shiva

**Shankhadhara** – bearer of the conch

**Shankhin** – Lord Vishnu

**Shaantanu** – a king in the epic of Mahabharata

**Shaanti** – peace

**Sharad** – winter

**Sharadchandrikaa** – Moon shine

**Sharvara** – Kamdeva

**Shashi** – Moon

**Shashira** – cool

**Shaashvata** – eternal, immortal

**Shatendra** – one who possesses hundred senses

**Shatimanyu** – Lord Indra

**Shatrujeeta** – one who conquers enemy

**Shatrunjaya** – one who overcomes enemy

**Sheela** – conduct

**Sheelanidhi** – treasury of good conduct

**Sheetala** – cold

**Shekhara** – crown

**Sheshanaaga** – king of serpent

**Shewetaketu** – white bannered

**Shikhandee** – son of Drupada

**Shikhara** – a top summit

**Shikhin** – peacock

**Shinendra** – Lord Shiva and Indra

**Shireesha** – name of a tree

**Shishu** – child

**Shitikantha** – Lord Shiva

**Shiva** – Lord Shiva

**Shoore** – brave

**Shorya** – bravery

**Shraavana** – lunar month

**Shrdhaananda** – devotee

**Shreya** – better, credit

**Shrutakeerti** – a person who is very famous

**Shubh** – auspicious

**Shubhaashisha** – blessing

**Shuchendra** – Lord of purity

**Shukla** – silver

**Shutottama** – best among the brave

**Shwitaan** – white

**Shyam** – Lord Krishna

**Siddhishwara** – Lord Shiva

**Sitaamshu** – Moon

**Skanda** – Lord Shiva

**Sohana** – handsome

**Somdeva** – Moon-god

**Stimita** – calm

**Subandhu** – closely related

**Subhaga** – blessed

**Subodha** – very patient

**Sudipta** – shining
**Sugreeve** – one of the Sun horses
**Suhaasa** – a person having a lovely smile
**Sukesha** – who possesses beautiful hair
**Sukumar** – delicate
**Sumantra** – good advice
**Sumegha** – well clouded
**Sumeru** – a name of a mountain
**Sumesha** – a king of flower
**Sumitra** – good friend
**Sundar** – beautiful

**Surashreshta** – Lord Vishnu
**Sureshvara** – Lord Indra
**Surya** – the Sun
**Surkanta** – the light of the Sun
**Suveera** – having a brave offspring
**Suvrata** – very religious
**Suyodhana** – excellent warrior
**Swaroopa** – similar
**Swapanna** – dream
**Swaraja** – freedom
**Swatantra** – independent
**Swayambhu** – self existence
**Swedesh** – own country

# T

**Taaraachand** - silver star

**Taaraka** – a star

**Taareesh** – the ocean

**Taarendra** – the star, prince

**Tajeshwara** – the Sun

**Takshaka** – a carpenter

**Tamoghna** – the Sun, destroyer of darkness

**Tamohara** – the Moon

**Tanmaya** – engrossed

**Tanya** – son

**Tapana** – the son

**Tapas** – heat

**Tapasendra** – Lord Shiva

**Tapaspati** – Lord of austerites

**Tapodyuti** – a person who is bright in religious merits

**Tapomaya** – virtuous

**Taponidhi** – a pious person

**Tarana** – heaven

**Taranga** – wave

**Tarika** – one who crosses the river of life

**Taru** – tree

**Tarun** – a young man

**Tasmin** – literally

**Tathagata** – Lord Buddha

**Teekshanarashmi** – the Sun

**Teertha** – holy place

**Tejapaal** – protector of lustre

**Tejas** – sharpness

**Tejaswi** – one who penances

**Tejomaya** – glorious
**Thyaagraaja** – a famous music composer
**Tilaka** – mark made on the forehead with Chandan
**Timin** – a large fish
**Timir** – night
**Tittiri** – the partridge
**Toshaka** – one who is happy
**Tribhuvana** – three worlds
**Trimoorti** – Brahma, Vishnu & Maheshwara
**Trinetra** – three eyed, Lord Shiva
**Tripura** – confluence of three cities
**Trishanku** – a king of Ayodhaya
**Trivikrama** – Lord Vishnu
**Triyambaka** – three eyed
**Tuhina** – very cold
**Tulaadhara** – the holder of the scales
**Tulsidaasa** – servant of basil
**Tungara** – high
**Tungesha** – the Moon
**Tungisha** – Lord Shiva
**Tureeya** – soul's fourth state
**Tushaara** – cold
**Tvashta** – the carpenter
**Twesha** – bright
**Tayaachaarya** – preceptor

# U

**Uchchdeva** – Lord Shiva

**Uchchhala** – upward rise of a spring

**Udadhi** – the ocean

**Udatta** – generous

**Uday** – rising high

**Udayachal** – eastern horizon

**Udayamaana** – accomplishment

**Udbhasa** – lusture

**Udbhava** – creation, origin

**Udbuddha** – awakened

**Uddhava** – name of a yadav king

**Uddipta** – lighted

**Uddisha** – Lord Shiva

**Udeepa** – flood

**Udgata** – to summon a deity by enchanted mantras

**Udghata** – to show

**Udghosha** – proclaiming

**Udgriva** – raised head

**Udhyoti** – the Sun

**Udit** – risen

**Udyaana** – garden

**Ugagria** – the high peak

**Ugraayudha** – one who uses dreadful weapons

**Ugradeva** – the terrible god

**Ugrashekhar** – Lord Shiva

**Ugrayaayi** – one who walks fiercely

**Ugresha** – Lord Shiva

**Ujaas** – light

**Ujagara** – bright

**Ujala** – bright

**Ujesha** – giver of light
**Ujjawal** – clean
**Ulhaasa** – joyous
**Ulind** – Lord Shiva
**Ullasa** – happiness
**Ulmukha** – curious
**Umaasee** – generous
**Umadaa** – the best
**Umakant** – Lord Shiva
**Umanga** – happiness
**Umaprasad** – blessing of Parvati
**Umarao** – noble
**Umashankara** – Lord Shiva
**Umeda** – hope
**Umesha** – Lord Shiva
**Unmatta** – excited
**Unmesha** – opening
**Unmilana** – expanding
**Upadhaya** – the teacher

**Upaasi** – a person who is fasting
**Upavana** – the Garden
**Upendra** – Lord Vishnu
**Uphaara** – the gift
**Urvidhara** – mountain
**Ushakaant** – Lord of the dawn
**Utkarna** – having the ears erect
**Utkarsh** – eminent
**Utkrusht** – the best
**Utpala** – lotus, water lily
**Utphala** – the best fruit
**Utsanga** – embrace
**Utsarga** – desirous
**Utsuka** – eager
**Uttama** – the best
**Uttang** – himalayas
**Utthana** – to rise

# V

**Vadeka** – Indra
**Vaachaspati** – God of speech
**Vachan** – oath
**Vadulee** – Vishwamitra's son
**Vaibhava** – wealth
**Vaihayaas** – aerial
**Vajree** – Lord Indra
**Vallabha** – beloved
**Valmiki** – a sage who wrote famous epic Ramayana
**Vamana** – Lord Vishnu
**Varuna** – God of ocean
**Vashishtha** – a famous sage
**Vashu** – God
**Vatsee** – Lord Vishnu
**Vedaprakash** – light of knowledge
**Vedhaa** – Lord Brahma
**Venimashava** – Lord Krishna
**Vibhakar** – the Sun
**Vibhat** – the dawn
**Vibhu** – one who is everywhere
**Vibhuda** – Moon
**Vidhu** – Moon
**Vidyadhar** – learned person
**Vidyadhip** – Lord Shiva
**Vidyakara** – seeker of knowledge
**Vidyasagar** – ocean of learning
**Vidyesh** – Lord Shiva
**Vikas** – progress, development
**Vikesh** – the Moon
**Vikram** – Lord Vishnu

**Vikramaditya** – a famous king, second to none in bravery

**Vikranta** – courageous

**Vilakshna** – celestial

**Viloka** – to see

**Vimal** – clear

**Vinaya** – modesty

**Vinod** – joy

**Vipasa** – a river

**Vipin** – jungle

**Vipla** – abundance

**Virthya** – Lord Shiva

**Vishala** – huge

**Vishambhar** – a supreme being

**Vishesha** – special

**Vishnu** – executor of the world

**Vishvadeva** – the Lord of the universe

**Vishwasa** – trust

**Vitesh** – Kubera

**Vithalaa** – Lord Vishnu

**Viveka** – wise

**Vrajesh** – Lord Krishna

**Vyas** – a famous sage who wrote Mahabharata

# W-X-Y-Z

**Wahab** – big hearted
**Wajidali** – involved
**Wali** – protector
**Yaadevandra** – Lord Krishna
**Yaaja** – a person belonging to high class Brahmin family
**Yaatree** – traveller
**Yadav** – a person who belongs to Yadu clan
**Yadunandana** – Lord Krishna
**Yadunath** – Lord Krishna
**Yagna** – sacrifice
**Yagnanga** – part of the sacrifice
**Yagnesha** – Lord of the sacrificial fire
**Yaksha** – a class of demi-god

**Yakshandraa** – Kuber
**Yakshraaj** – Kuber
**Yakshesha** – Kuber
**Yakshpati** – Kuber
**Yama** – the Lord of death
**Yamadoot** – the messenger of death
**Yamaraaja** – Lord of death
**Yamula** – twin, pair
**Yashaschanra** – Moon of glory
**Yashaskaama** – a person who desires to attain fame
**Yashaskara** – famous
**Yashawanta** – attainment of glory
**Yashodhana** – very famous
**Yashomitra** – a friend of fame

**Yashpal** – famous
**Yateendra** – one who is able to control his passion
**Yatesha** – Lord of ascetic
**Yati** – a devotee
**Yatin** – an ascetic
**Yayaati** – a famous king in Puranas
**Yogendra** – Lord of Yoga
**Yogesh** – Lord Krishna
**Yogeshawara** – one who attains superhuman power
**Yogin** – a person who possesses magical powers
**Yudhajita** – victorious in war

**Yudhaveera** – a great warrior
**Yudhistera** – one who is fair in war
**Yugal** – pair
**Yugal Kishore** – Radha Krishna
**Yuvaraala** – prince
**Yuyutsu** – one who wishes to fight
**Zachariah** – God's remembrance
**Zafar** – achievement
**Zahid** – intelligent
**Zain** – good light
**Zaki** – saintly
**Zaurashtra** – parsee God
**Zoravar** – brave
**Zubair** – pure
**Zuber** – pure

# Names for Baby Girl

# A

**Aabha** – light
**Aabharika** – gratitude, one who has halo
**Aadhya** – one of ten forms of Durga
**Aaditi** – the Earth
**Aahaldita** – a woman who is happy
**Aakaanksha** – desire
**Aakarshana** – attraction
**Aakriti** – shape
**Aakraanti** – force
**Aakuti** – intention
**Aalaapini** – a singer
**Aamodini** – fragrance
**Aamrapali** – leaf of mango tree
**Aamrapallavi** – leaf of mango tree
**Aanandaprana** – a woman of joy
**Aanandita** – a happy person who spreads joy
**Aanandi** – always happy
**Aanandini** – giver of joy
**Aaradhana** – worship
**Aarohee** – a creeper
**Aarati** – to worship
**Aarunika** – tawny red
**Aashankita** – full of hope
**Aashika** – beloved
**Aashivini** – egoist
**Aavriti** – repeat
**Abhidhaa** – sound
**Abhaya** – fearless
**Abhijayaa** – victory
**Abhijitaa** – conquered

**Abhilasha** – desire
**Abhilashini** – full of desire
**Abhimaneenee** – self respected woman
**Abhinandni** – one who delights
**Abhinandita** – one who delights
**Abhirupaa** – beautiful
**Abhisaarika** – a person who keeps trust of beloved
**Abhivandana** – to salute
**Abuditaa** – awakened
**Achalaa** – the Earth
**Achiraa** – one who is fresh with beauty
**Adattaa** – unmarried girl
**Aditi** – nature, the Earth
**Adrijaa** – daughter of mountain

**Adwrika** – small mountain
**Adwitiyaa** – a unique woman
**Aganiya** – uncommon
**Agnayi** – Goddess of fire
**Agnivadhu** – wife of fire
**Agnivesha** – the Sun
**Ahalaya** – wife of Gautam Rishi
**Aina** – belonging to black doe
**Airavati** – name of river
**Aishani** – Goddess Durga
**Aishvarya** – luxury
**Akashara** – alphabets, eternal
**Akhandita** – unbroken
**Akhilaa** – entire
**Akshaya** – Imperishable
**Akshayni** – immortal

**Akshayee** – undecaying

**Akshataa** – unmarried woman

**Alopaa** – free from desires

**Alpana** – decorative design

**Alakhnandaa** – a young girl

**Alankrita** – decorated

**Aamalua** – name of Ganga river

**Ambujaa** – Goddess Lakshmi

**Ameetaa** – boundless, without limit

**Ambaa** – mother

**Ambikaa** – mothar goddess

**Amitaa** – boundless

**Amiyaa** – nectar

**Amritaa** – immortal

**Amritalata** – a nectar giving creeper

**Amodini** – joyful

**Amoghasiddhi** – one who does not fail

**Amishaa** – honest

**Amishi** – honest

**Amurshaa** – truth

**Amulya** – priceless

**Anangalekha** – letter written from heart

**Anangmalini** – garland of Lord Kama

**Ananadini** – joyful

**Anandi** – a person who gives joy

**Anantaa** – eternal

**Ananatdevee** – eternal goddess

**Ananyaa** – the only one

**Anasuyaa** – one without any bad feelings

**Anganaa** – woman with beautiful limb

**Angalekha** – a creeper

**Angoori** – bright, like grape
**Aneeshaa** – supreme
**Anishaa** – continuous
**Anekta** – diversity
**Aniketa** – homeless
**Anjali** – homage
**Anjana** – a mountain
**Anjanee** – adorn with sandalwood paste
**Anjushree** – a beautiful woman who adorns herself
**Ankita** – written
**Anaamika** – without a name
**Annapurana** – the goddess of crop
**Anshumala** – garland of rays
**Anshumalinia** – garland of rays
**Antrikshaa** – the sky
**Anubhuti** – experience
**Anujaa** – younger
**Anulekha** – born later

**Anumati** – permission
**Anupriya** – like beloved,uncomparable
**Anuradhaa** – like Radha
**Anupsara** – beautiful woman
**Anupmaa** – beautiful woman, incomparable
**Anurati** – full of affection
**Anuttmaa** – best of all
**Anuttraa** – without answer
**Anuvidyaa** – to gain knowledge
**Anvikshaa** – to give
**Anvitaa** – one who bridges the gap
**Aparajitaa** – unconquered, Parvati, goddess
**Aparnaa** – leafless
**Apekshaa** – expectation

**Apoorvaa** – very beautiful

**Apoorvee** – supreme soul

**Apsaraa** – beautiful woman

**Aranyanee** – Goddess of food

**Aradhanaa** – worship

**Archanaa** – one who adores

**Architaa** – one who is honoured

**Arjitaa** – one who has given away

**Arpita** – one who is dedicated

**Aruna** – morning, the dawn

**Arvindaa** – lotus

**Aseemaa** – unlimited

**Arshia** – heavenly

**Arundhati** – a star

**Ashna** – friend

**Asitaa** – river Yamuna

**Asteshaa** – a star

**Asmitaa** – pride

**Atreyi** – pride

**Atulyaa** – matchless

**Avani** – Earth

**Avanti** – name of city

**Avantikaa** – people reside in Avanti city

**Avinashnee** – one who cannot be destroyed

# B

**Baageshree** – beauty, Saraswati

**Baahulee** – full Moon in the month of Kartik

**Baani** – speech

**Babhravee** – another name of Durga

**Badrika** – source of river Ganga

**Bakulavali** – string of Bakula flower

**Bakulamalaa** – necklace of Bhakul flower

**Balapradaa** – strength giver

**Balaprasoo** – Rohini, mother of Balram

**Banamala** – a garland of flowers

**Bansi** – flute

**Banitaa** – a woman

**Bansuri** – flute

**Barkhaa** – Ram

**Basanti** – spring season

**Balchandrikaa** – woman, beautiful like Moon

**Bayjayanti** – a garland of Lord Vishnu

**Beejali** – light

**Belaa** – a flower

**Beenaa** – intelligence, a lute, musical instrument

**Bhaagyaa** – prosperity

**Bhaagya-Lakshmi** – Lakshmi who brings prosperity

**Bhaageerathi** – the Ganga

**Bhaagvati** – fortunate woman

**Bhaagvanti** – fortunate woman

**Bhamini** – a woman

{94}

**Bhaanavee** – daughter of Bhaanu

**Bhaanushree** – beautiful woman

**Bhaanumati** – beautiful, skillful

**Bhaanusuta** – woman, daughter of the Sun

**Bhaavnaa** – faith, desire

**Bhaarti** – Goddess of speech

**Bhaargavi** – daughter of the Sun

**Bhaavika** – natural

**Bhaavinee** – a noble lady

**Bhadrikaa** – beautiful noble lady

**Bhadrakshi** – one with a beautiful face

**Bhadramukhi** – one with beautiful eyes

**Bhadralee** – beautiful female friend

**Bhadrapriyaa** – lover

**Bhagvatee** – name of Lakshmi and Durga

**Bhairavi** – the goddess Durga in infuriated form

**Bhajnandini** – Goddess

**Bhakti** – devotion

**Bhanvaree** – name of woman

**Bhanupriyaa** – beloved of Sun

**Bhanujaa** – daughter of Sun

**Bhavaambee** – mother of good woman

**Bhavani** – Goddess Parvati

**Bhaumika** – associated with Earth

**Bhav-vama** – Paravati

**Bhavana** – feeling

**Bhilangana** – a river

**Bhavnoor** – out of this world

**Bhringi** – an attendent of Lord Shiva

**Bhuvaneshvaree** – name of Durga

**Bhuvandevee** – Goddess of the world

**Bhooritaa** – abundance

**Bhogvati** – one who gives the pleasure

**Bhoorik** – the Earth

**Bhoosutaa** – Sita

**Bhoomijaa** – daughter of the Earth

**Bhuvi** – the Earth

**Bimbikaa** – the disc of Moon

**Binaa** – musical instrument

**Bindyaa** – a droplet

**Bindu** – a drop, dot

**Bindulekhaa** – name of woman

**Bindumalini** – pearl garlanded

**Bindumatee** – a small particle

**Bineetaa** – one who is humble

**Binodini** – full of recreation

**Buddhi** – reason, intellectual

**Bodhvati** – learned woman

**Brijaanganaa** – woman of Brija

**Brindaa** – name of Radha

**Bulbul** – name of a bird

# C

**Chaamunda** – fierce form of Durga

**Chaandni** – Moonlight

**Chaaru** – beloved

**Chaarungi** – beautiful woman

**Chaarudarshanaa** – beautiful to look

**Chaarudatta** – very charming

**Chaarudhara** – Indra's wife

**Chaarukesha** – a woman with beautiful hair

**Chaarulochna** – a woman with beautiful eyes

**Chaarumati** – intelligent woman

**Chaaruvardhana** – a woman whose beauty increases day by day

**Chaaruvakee** – name of a queen

**Chaaruveni** – with beautiful hair

**Chaarvi** – splendour

**Chakrini** – potter

**Chameli** – jasmine

**Champa** – a flower

**Champa Kali** – a bud of Champa

**Champaka** – a tree with yellow fragrant flower

**Champakmalaa** – a garland of Champa flower

**Champavarnee** – one who has complexion of Champa flower

**Champaavati** – ever-fragrant

**Chanchalaa** – the goddess of wealth, unsteady

**Chandana** – sandal wood

**Chanda** – Moon

**Chandani** – Moon light

**Chandanika** – a small sandalwood tree

**Chandan Gandha** – a fragrance of sandalwood

**Chandikaa** – name of Durga

**Chandalini** – glorious

**Chandiraa** – the Moon

**Chandranshu** – a Moon beam

**Chandrajaa** – a Moon beam

**Chandramani** – Moonstone

**Chandra Jyoti** – Moon light

**Chandralee** – Friend of Moon

**Chandrikaa** – The Moon lit

**Chandrakalaa** – a woman expert in lunar art

**Chandra Kanta** – wife of Moon

**Chandra Mallika** – jasmine

**Chandra Prabha** – the Moon lit

**Chandra Mukhi** – a woman beautiful like Moon

**Chandra Rekha** – ray of Moon

**Chandraani** – round faced

**Chandrasheda** – soft, gentle

**Chandra Vadanee** – Moon faced

**Chandravali** – like Moon

**Chandra Vallabhaa** – beloved of Moon

**Chandravati** – illuminated by Moon

**Chandree** – Moon light

{98}

**Chandrimaa** – the Moon

**Chantni** – beloved

**Chaplaa** – lightening

**Changla** – a musical note

**Chanchalaa** – agile

**Chhali** – a kind of creeper

**Chhavi** – beauty, image

**Chhayaa** – shadow

**Chhinnamastaa** – a name of Durga

**Cheshtaa** – joke

**Chetnaa** – wisdom, consciousness

**Chintani** – meditation

**Chiti** – knowledge

**Chitraa** – beautiful woman's portrait

**Chitralekha** – an artist

**Chitrinee** – talented woman

**Chitrakeshi** – a woman with beautiful hair

**Chitramayi** – like a portrait

**Chitraangi** – a woman with lovely body

**Chitshakti** – intellectual

**Chit Shaanti** – eternal peace of mind

**Chudaamani** – head jewel

# D

**Daamini** – lightening
**Dadhijaa** – as soft as butter
**Dakshaa** – intelligent
**Dakshajaa** – Goddess Durga
**Dakshakanyaa** – Goddess Durga
**Dakshee** – intelligent
**Dakshyani** – Goddess Durga
**Dhamvati** – Damyanti
**Damyanti** – a woman from Puranas
**Dandagauri** – Goddess Durga
**Darni** – Goddess Durga
**Darpanaa** – looking glass
**Darpinee** – proud
**Darpitaa** – proud
**Darshana** – vision

**Darshanaa** – good looking
**Darshee** – percieved
**Darshitaa** – to show
**Darvikaa** – sacrificial spoon
**Dashamee** – the tenth day of lunar month
**Dasharna** – a name of the river
**Dashbhujaa** – one who has ten hands, Goddess Durga
**Dasheya** – Satyawati
**Dattadevee** – Goddess of Boons
**Dayaa** – pity, sympathy
**Dayaasheela** – sympathic
**Dayitaa** – lover
**Deeksha** – consecreation

**Deepaa** – lustrous woman

**Deepaalikaa** – flame of light

**Deepaali** – row of lights

**Deepak** – light giver

**Deepikaa** – one who leads the way

**Deepshikhaa** – lamp's flame

**Deeptaa** – bright woman

**Deepti** – splendour

**Devaganikaa** – a nymph

**Devaharshaa** – the happiness of God

**Devahuti** – daughter of Manu

**Devakee** – mother of Lord Krishna

**Devalaa** – a woman attendant of the idol of God

**Devamaatri** – mother of God

**Devanganaa** – a celestial woman

**Devanjaa** – a lady who has knowledge of God

**Devaprabhaa** – divine light

**Devarati** – celestial woman

**Devasree** – divine beauty

**Devavaani** – divine voice

**Devayaani** – daughter of the guru Shukraachaaryaa

**Deveenaa** – wife of God

**Devikaa** – derived from God

**Dhaaraa** – stream of water

**Dhaarinee** – Earth

**Dhaaritree** – Earth

**Dhaatri** – a nurse

**Dhairyabaalaa** – a woman with courage

**Dhanadaa** – Goddess of wealth

**Dhanasri** – glory of wealth

**Dhanavidyaa** – wealth of knowledge

**Dhaneshwari** – Goddess of wealth

**Dhanurjaya** – charm of wealth

**Dhanya** – great

**Dhanyaa** – virtuous

**Dharaa** – Earth

**Dharani** – Earth

**Dharitree** – Earth

**Dharmishtaa** – faith in religion

**Dhavala** – one who possesses fair complexion

**Dhavani** – fire

**Dheeraa** – control of senses

**Dhenumati** – river Gomti

**Dhritaa** – patience

**Dhrumana** – firm mind

**Dhruvadevee** – a name of a princess

**Dhundhalee** – one who does not have a child

**Digamberee** – naked woman

**Dishaa** – direction

**Dishti** – fortunate

**Diti** – dividing

**Divyaa** – divine, heavenly

**Divyamberee** – dressed in heavenly manner

**Diwaalee** – the festival of light

**Drashtaa** – an onlooker

**Drishti** – sight

**Draupadee** – wife of five Pandavas

**Dulaaree** – lovable

**Durga** – mercy

**Durgee** – one who lives in the fort

**Dweepaa** – she elephant

**Dwipaadee** – with two legs

**Dyumanhuti** – inspired

**Dyuti** – bright

# E

**Eashaa** – desire, Devi Durga

**Edha** – prosperity

**Eehita** – desired

**Eekshita** – the sight

**Eeravati** – name of river

**Eeshavarkantaa** – name of Durga

**Eera** – the wind

**Eeraja** – wwind born

**Eda** – the praise

**Ekaa** – unity

**Ekataa** – unity

**Ekaakita** – loneliness

**Ekaavali** – string of pearls

**Ekinee** – one who is alone

**Ekshan** – philosophy

**Ekodaraa** – sister

**Ela** – creepers name

**Elaa** – cardamom

**Elokeshee** – eyes like ela creeper

**Enakshee** – doe-eyed

**Eni** – black doe

**Eshanaa** – desire

**Eshanadevi** – name of woman

**Eshaanee** – Devi Durga

**Eshvari** – Goddess

**Eshvaryaa** – the prosperity

**Eshika** – the eye

# G

**Gaatha** – story written in verse, poem

**Gaayatree** – name of a very sacred mantra

**Gaayatreenee** – one who sings hymns

**Gabhasti** – ray, light

**Gaganaangnaa** – celestial woman

**Gaganasindhu** – Ganga river

**Gajagaminee** – a woman of stately, elephant like gait

**Gajagati** – as graceful as elephant gait

**Gajal** – urdu poem

**Gajalakshmi** – Lakshmi flanked by tuskers

**Gajamani** – jewel of an elephant

**Gajamuktaa** – jewel on forehead of an elephant

**Gajapushpee** – name of a creeper

**Gajara** – wreath of flowers

**Gambheeraa** – depth, name of a river

**Gambheerikaa** – name of a river

**Gandhaa** – a sweet smelling woman

**Gandharvee** – celestial musician and dancer

**Gandharvapadaa** – a Gandharva girl

**Gandharvakanya** – a virgin woman

**Gandharikaa** – a person who prepares perfumes

**Gandhaavati** – the Earth

**Gandhalataa** – a creeper with fragrance

**Gandhamaalince** – strong scented

**Gandhashekhara** – musk

**Gandhavallari** – a fragrant creeper

**Ganavati** – name of Parwati

**Ganga** – name of a River

**Gangotri** – a place from where Ganga originates

**Gargi** – daughter of sage Garg

**Garimaa** – greatness, dignity

**Garvitaa** – proud woman

**Gati** – speed

**Gatitaa** – a river

**Gauraangana** – fair complexioned

**Gauri** – Parvati, Rishi Gautam's wife

**Gavana Gautmi** – upper garment of a saree

**Gaveshnaa** – discovery

**Geerna** – famous

**Geeta** – a song

**Geeti** – singing

**Geetikaa** – a short poetry

**Gehini** – house-wife

**Ghantikaa** – a small bell

**Ghanaavalli** – creper of cloud

**Ghanaanjani** – a dark cloud

**Ghrani** – a ray of light

**Ghritaachi** – name of Saraswati

**Ghritavati** – name of River

**Ghoshavati** – Veena, lute

**Ghoshanin** – famed

**Ghoshanaa** – declaration

**Ghungroo** – dancer's wear for feet

**Ghunghari** – bracelet with jingling bells

**Giraa** – speech

**Giribaalaa** – daughter of mountain

**Giriganga** – name of the River

**Girijaa** – Parvati

**Girinandani** – Ganga, Parvati

**Giritanyaa** – daughter of mountain

**Girijatanyaa** – daughter of Parvati

**Gitaanjali** – a famous poem by Rabindranath Tagore, an anthology of poems

**Gitasudha** – sweet music

**Godhuli** – dust of the Earth raised by cows

**Gokanyaa** – maid who looks after cows

**Gopi** – cowherdess

**Gobindi** – Krishna's concert

**Godaavari** – a river

**Gomati** – a river

**Gopee** – milkmaid

**Gopalee** – maid of cowheard

**Gopika** – herdswoman

**Goraandi** – fair complexioned

**Gormaa** – gauri, fair

**Goshti** – conversation

**Gotamee** – Ahilaya, Gautam Rishi's wife

**Govindee** – Krishna's concert

**Gowrangi** – fair complexioned

**Gramakaali** – Goddess Kali of the village

**Grihalakshmi** – the Lakshmi of the house

**Grihini** – house wife
**Grihastini** – house wife
**Gulaab** – rose
**Gulaabee** – rosy
**Gulaal** – reddish powder
**Gudaakesha** – one who has conquered sleep
**Gunasundri** – the supreme being

**Gunavatee** – a virtuous woman
**Gunaavanti** – a virtuous woman
**Guniyal** – a virtuous woman
**Gunjana** – humming
**Gunjaa** – a small shrub with red and black berry
**Gyanada** – Goddess Saraswati

# H

**Hamid** – in praise of God

**Hamsamaalaa** – a flight of swans

**Hansavati** – beautiful woman

**Hansika** – little swan

**Hansgamini** – walk like swan

**Hansja** – river Yamuna

**Hansmukh** – smiling, cheerful

**Hansee** – a female swan

**Hansnandni** – with slender waist

**Hansinee** – swan

**Harabala** – daughter of Shiva

**Hara Devi** – Parvati

**Hanumatee** – name of a woman

**Hari Devi** – Parvati

**Harimani** – jewel

**Harinakshi** – doe eyed

**Harini** – doe

**Hari Priya** – Lakshmi

**Harita** – beautiful damsel

**Harshmati** – full of joy

**Harshni** – joyful

**Harshita** – full of joy

**Harshveena** – musical instrument

**Hastinee** – elephant

**Hasumati** – happy

**Heena** – fragrance

**Heera** – diamond

**Hema** – a kind of plant, golden

**Hemadauta** – a celestial damsel

**Hemangee** – one having a shining body

**Hemaketki** – the Ketki plant

**Hemamala** – consert of Yama

**Hemalata** – golden creeper

**Hemamalini** – golden flowers

**Hemanti** – shining like gold

**Hemantika** – of the winter season

**Hemaprabha** – golden lustre

**Hemapushpa** – golden flower

**Hemavaran** – golden complexion

**Hemna** – musical note

**Hemvati** – Parvati

**Hima** – ice, snow

**Himani** – mass of snow

**Himsuta** – Parvati

**Hina** – wheatish complexion

**Hiranyamayee** – golden

**Holika** – sister of Hiranyakush

**Hridayaa** – heart

**Hridyesha** – beloved

**Hridyasudha** – nectar of heart

**Hrishi** – happiness

**Hrishiti** – pleasure

# I

**Ibhi** – an elephant
**Idaa** – speech
**Ijayaa** – sacrifice
**Ikshaa** – sight
**Ikshikaa** – a glance
**Ikshita** – to be seen
**Ikshudaa** – name of the river
**Ikshumaalin** – a florist, name of a river
**Ikshumati** – river in Kurushetra
**Ikshumatee** – possessor of sugarcane
**Ilaa** – speech, fish
**Ileshaa** – Lord of the Earth
**Ina** – mother
**Indira** – Goddess of wealth, Lakshmi
**Indalee** – to be powerful

**Indivaraprabha** – beauty of blue lotus
**Indivaraksha** – lotus eyed
**Indivarini** – a group of blue lotus
**Indrabaalaa** – daughter of Indra
**Indrabhagini** – sister of Indra
**Indraakshi** – beautiful eyed
**Indraani** – wife of Indra
**Indrapushpaa** – name of a plant which has medicinal value
**Indu** – Moonlight
**Indubhaa** – constellation's name
**Indujaa** – daughter of Indra, river Narmada

**Indulekha** – the Moon

**Indumala** – the blossom of white lotus

**Indumati** – consort of Moon

**Induprabhaa** – the light of the Moon

**Indurekha** – the rays of the Moon-light

**Indushekhara** – Moon

**Ipsa** – desire

**Ipsita** – desire

**Iraa** – The Earth

**Irikaa** – The Earth

**Ishaa** – Devi Durga

**Ishanee** – Devi Durga

**Ishani** – Parvati

**Ishnaa** – desire

**Ishita** – prosperity, the Goddess

**Ishwari** – Goddess

**Ishwarakaanta** – Durga

**Iti** – accomplished

# J

**Jaalandhara** – net

**Jaanavee** – epithet of the river Ganga

**Jaanki** – Sita

**Jagadambaa** – Goddess Durga

**Jagadgauri** – fair complexioned

**Jagamohini** – one who captivates the universe

**Jaganamaatri** – mother of the world

**Jagatee** – Earth

**Jagdambikaa** – Goddess Durga

**Jahanara** – queen of the universe

**Jahnava** – Ganga river

**Jahnukanyaa** – Ganga

**Jalabaala** – daughter of a river

**Jalabaalikaa** – lightening

**Jaladhaaraa** – stream of water

**Jalaja** – lotus

**Jalajakshi** – lotus eyed

**Jalaneeli** – moss

**Jalini** – one who lives in water

**Jamuna** – river Yamuna

**Janaki** – wife of Rama, Sita

**Janaksutta** – daughter of Janak

**Janaktanayaa** – Janak's daughter

**Janani** – mother

**Janika** – generating

**Jaraa** – old age, wise

**Jaswanti** – famous woman

**Jayaa** – Goddess Durga

**Jayaadevee** – Goddess of victory

**Jayabheri** – victory drum

**Jayadaa** – victory giver

**Jayadurga** – name of Durga

**Jayalakshmi** – Goddess of victory

**Jayalalithaa** – Goddess Durga

**Jayamangala** – auspicious victory

**Jayanti** – birth

**Jayaprabhaa** – light of victory

**Jayapradaa** – giver of victory

**Jayaswaminee** – Goddess Durga

**Jayeetaa** – one who is successful

**Jeeva** – life, water, the Earth, the chord of arc

**Jeevanteeka** – flower

**Jhaanavikaa** – Ganges

**Jhankaar** – wweet sound of paayal

**Jhankaarinee** – murmur

**Jharna** – a stream

**Jhoomer** – ornaments

**Jivyaa** – livelihood

**Jnanadaa** – aupreme knowledge

**Jnapti** – intelligent

**Joshika** – bud

**Joshitaa** – a woman

**Juhi** – a name of flower with fragrance

**Jwaalaa** – the flame

**Jyesthaa** – elder

**Jyotibaalaa** – woman of flame

**Jyotikaa** – light

**Jyotilekhaa** – written with light

**Jyotishmati** – one attained enlightenment who has attained enlightenment

**Jyotsinaalataa** – creeper of Moonlight

**Jyotsnaa** – Moonlight

**Jyotsnee** – Moonlight

**Jyotsnikaa** – Moonlight

# K

**Kaadambari** – a river

**Kaahini** – young woman

**Kaakalee** – sweet

**Kaali** – Goddess Kali

**Kaalikaa** – group of clouds

**Kaalkingi** – Kalinga's woman

**Kaamaniyam** – beautiful

**Kaameshwari** – Goddess of desires

**Kaamini** – desirable, beautiful woman

**Kaanana** – orchard

**Kaankasha** – desire

**Kaanya** – lustre

**Kaayaayinee** – Goddess Parvati

**Kaaveree** – bangle

**Kadamabari** – cuckoo

**Kadambari** – flower of kadamb

**Kairavee** – Moon light

**Kairravini** – lotus plant

**Kaisara** – the queen

**Kajal** – kohl

**Kajari** – a woman with black eyes

**Kala** – art

**Kalawati** – a woman with knowledge of arts

**Kalayani** – blessed, prospered

**Kalika** – bud, Devi Durga

**Kalindi** – river Yamuna

**Kallol** – large waves

**Kallolee** – one who is happy

**Kalmashi** – river Yamuna

**Kalollini** – stream

**Kalpalata** – determination, secret wish

**Kalpanaa** – imagination

**Kalpikaa** – proper, dream

**Kalpitaa** – imaginative

**Kalyani** – Goddess

**Kamakashi** – Durga

**Kamalaa** – Lakshmi

**Kamalaakshi** – eyes like lotus

**Kamalalochnaa** – eyes like lotus

**Kaamanaa** – desire

**Kaamayani** – shradha, desire

**Kaameshwari** – Durga

**Kamini** – beautiful woman

**Kamniva** – beautiful

**Kanakaa** – gold

**Kanakvi** – small kite

**Kanchana** – gold

**Kanchi** – golden, waist band

**Kangana** – bangle

**Kanikaa** – an atom

**Kanishtha** – youngest

**Kanishthakaa** – little finger

**Kanjaree** – musical instrument

**Kanta** – earth, attractive woman

**Kanti** – beautiful

**Kanu Priya** – beloved of Krishna

**Kanwal** – lotus

**Kapalini** – Durga

**Kapardikaa** – shell

**Kapardini** – Durga, Goddess Parvati

**Kapilaa** – innocent woman

**Kapinjalaa** – a river

**Karanee** – action

**Kardami** – full Moon

**Karini** – elephant

**Karishmaa** – wonder
**Karunaa** – compassion
**Kashyapee** – Earth
**Kasturba** – a precious stone
**Kasturi** – musk
**Kaudambi** – the full Moonlight
**Kaumadi** – Moonlight
**Kaushalya** – mother of Lord Rama
**Kaushika** – love
**Kautki** – full of curiosity
**Kavita** – poetry
**Kesari** – saffron
**Khayaati** – fame
**Khushali** – happiness
**Kenneri** – demi-god
**Kiraati** – Goddess Parvati
**Kiran** – rays
**Kirati** – fame
**Kishori** – young woman

**Kokila** – cuckoo
**Komala** – tender, soft
**Komalaangi** – one who possesses tender body
**Krantee** – revolution
**Kripaa** – favour
**Kripee** – sister of Kripa
**Krishnee** – night with darkness
**Kriti** – creation
**Krushnee** – dark night
**Ksheerjaa** – Goddess of wealth, Lakshmi
**Kshemalataa** – creeper of welfare
**Kshemya** – Goddess Durga
**Kshipra** – fast
**Kshiti** – earth
**Kshitijaa** – horizon
**Kshma** – Goddess Durga, pardon
**Kumkum** – saffron
**Kumuda** – red lotus

**Kulaagnaa** – descended from noble family

**Kumudini** – a pond full of red lotus

**Kundanikaa** – creeper of jasmine

**Kunitala** – woman with long hair, lock of hair

**Kunti** – a bee, mother of Pandavas of Mahabharata

**Kusum** – flower

**Kusumita** – like a flower, blossomed

# L

**Laalasaa** – desire
**Laavanyamayi** – full of beauty
**Laghima** – lightness
**Lahara** – the wave
**Laj** – modesty
**Lajjaasheel** – modest woman
**Lajjawati** – modest woman
**Lajjettaa** – a shameful woman
**Lajwanti** – modest woman
**Lakhi** – bronze colour
**Laksha** – rose
**Lakshana** – symbol
**Lakshita** – symbolic
**Lakshmi** – Goddess of wealth
**Lakshmisaraswati** – Lakshmi and Saraswati
**Lalanaa** – a woman

**Lalanikaa** – caress
**Laalimaa** – redish colour
**Lalitaa** – attractive
**Lalitaalochan** – a woman with beautiful eyes
**Lalitangee** – a woman who possesses beautiful body
**Lasikaa** – dancer
**Lataa** – creeper
**Latakastureekaa** – musk creeper
**Latamani** – jewel
**Latikaa** – a small creeper
**Lavana** – the brightness
**Lavangalata** – clove creeper
**Lavangee** – clove plant

{119}

**Lavanikaa** – beautiful

**Lavanya** – graceful

**Lavleen** – absorbed

**Leela** – charming

**Leelawati** – Goddess Durga

**Leena** – involved with God

**Lekhaa** – writing

**Lepaakshi** – with painted eyes

**Lily** – a flower

**Lipi** – script

**Lochana** – the eyes

**Lolitaa** – person who is roving

**Lomaa** – a person with long hair

**Lopaa** – loss

**Lopamudraa** – Agastya Rishi's wife

**Lotikaa** – tearful person

**Lumbini** – a princess

# M

**Maalini** – a florist
**Maanini** – a proud woman
**Maatangi** – Parvati
**Madhu** – honey
**Madhulekha** – a girl as sweet as honey
**Madhulika** – honey
**Madhumakshita** – honey bee
**Madhumita** – honey
**Madhunisha** – night full of pleasure
**Madhup** – black bee
**Madhur** – sweet
**Madhuri** – wweet
**Madhurima** – beauty
**Madhvi** – spring
**Madirakshi** – intoxicated eyes
**Mahadevi** – Parvati
**Mahagauri** – Goddess Parvati

**Mahasweta** – Goddess Saraswati
**Maheshwati** – Goddess Durga
**Mahikaa** – the Earth
**Mahimaa** – fame
**Mahishi** – wife
**Mahua** – a flower
**Maina** – a bird
**Maithali** – Sita
**Maitrevi** – a learned woman
**Maitri** – friendship
**Makshi** – honey bee
**Makshika** – honey bee
**Maalaa** – garland
**Malaya** – name of a mountain
**Malhaara** – a musical instrument
**Mallikaa** – a creeper
**Malti** – a creeper

**Mamta** – motherly love

**Manalee** – a friend of mind

**Manasvinee** – a wise woman

**Mandaa** – name of a river

**Mandakni** – river Ganga

**Mandiraa** – a dwelling

**Mandodri** – name of Ravana's wife

**Mandra** – sober

**Mandva** – mandap

**Mandyanti** – Goddess Durga

**Mangla** – Goddess Parvati

**Maanikya** – a jewel

**Maanini** – Respectful

**Maanisha** – intelligent woman

**Manishikaa** – desire of the mind

**Manjaarikaa** – bud

**Manjari** – pearl, new tendril

**Manjukeshee** – one with beautiful hair

**Manjula** – beautiful

**Manjusha** – a box

**Manjyot** – light of the mind

**Manka** – a wooden pearl

**Manoharita** – beautiful

**Manoritaa** – beauty

**Manorma** – beautiful

**Mansa** – desire

**Mansha** – desire

**Mansi** – a Goddess

**Manthra** – property

**Mantra** – a divine prayer

**Manushi** – about woman

**Manvi** – lady

**Maraalikaa** – small swan

**Mirachka** – attraction

**Matangi** – an intellectual

**Matseyagandha** – a lady who smells like a fish

**Matsya** – fish

**Maulikaa** – original

**Mausmi** – monsoon wind

**Maaya** – illusion

**Mayavani** – creating illusion

**Mayure** – peahen

**Meena** – precious stone

**Meenakshi** – woman with beautiful eyes

**Meera** – a saintly woman, one who is circumscribed

**Meeta** – a friend

**Meghal** – cloud

**Meghna** – cloud

**Mehaa** – rain

**Mekhla** – girdle

**Menaa** – name of a bird

**Meneka** – apsara (beautiful maiden from heaven)

**Mihikaa** – mist

**Mitraa** – friend

**Mohanaa** – fascinating

**Mohanagee** – a woman with attractive figure

**Mohini** – attractive

**Mohitaa** – enchanted

**Moksha** – salvation

**Monaa** – alone

**Mridu** – soft, sweet

**Mridula** – softness, sweetness

**Mrigakshi** – beautiful eyes like deer

**Mriglochni** – beautiful eyes like deer

**Mrignayani** – with beautiful eyes like deer

**Mrigtrishna** – mirage

**Mrigya** – deer

**Mrinal** – delicate

**Mrinalinee** – doe eyed

**Mrinalini** – lotus

**Mrinallika** – stalk of lotus

**Mrudaanee** – Parvati

**Mrugaa** – doe

**Mrugakshi** – doe eyed

**Muditaa** – delighted person

**Mudra** – pose

**Mudraa** – seal

**Mugdha** – absorbed

**Mugdhaa** – attractive

**Mukta** – free

**Muktaa** – pearl

**Muktavali** – necklace of pearl

**Mukti** – salvation

**Myna** – a black bird which sings beautifully

**Magan** – engrossed

**Mahi** – Earth

**Megha** – a star

# N

**Naayikaa** – actress
**Naaz** – pride
**Nabhaswati** – creator of noise in sky
**Nagaja** – mountain born
**Nagina** – jewel
**Naina** – eyes
**Nakshtramalaa** – chain of star
**Nalinakshi** – lotus eyed
**Nalini** – river
**Namita** – humble
**Namrataa** – modesty
**Nanda** – joyful
**Nandini** – Ganga
**Narayani** – Goddess Lakshmi
**Nargis** – a name of yellow flower
**Navoditaa** – new
**Nayanataraa** – eyes like a star
**Naynaa** – eyes
**Nazima** – song
**Neelakshi** – blue eyed
**Neelam** – blue sapphire
**Neelambaree** – one who wears blue clothes
**Neelanjanaa** – black surma
**Neerjaa** – lotus
**Neeta** – wells-behaved
**Neeti** – conduct
**Nehaa** – affectionate
**Netraa** – eyes
**Nibhaa** – light
**Nidhi** – treasure
**Nihaara** – mist
**Niharikaa** – heavy dew
**Nijaa** – one's very own

**Nikashaa** – mother of Ravanaa
**Nikunja** – bower
**Nimilaa** – pretend
**Nimilikaa** – closed eyes
**Nipunaa** – expert
**Niraalee** – exceptional
**Nireekshaa** – to search
**Nirjaa** – clean

**Nirupmaa** – Gayatri
**Nisha** – night
**Nishchalaa** – steady
**Nishi** – night
**Nishita** – night
**Nishitha** – devotion
**Nityaa** – constant, Goddess Durga
**Niveditaa** – offer of God, teacher
**Niyati** – fate
**Nupur** – the anklet
**Nutan** – new

**Oshdhi** – medicine
**Ojadaa** – strengthening
**Ojasbala** – Goddess of Bodhi tree
**Ojasvini** – lustrous

**Ojasvitaa** – lustrous woman
**Omana** – a woman
**Omvati** – sacred
**Oorja** – energy
**Oormi** – current

# P

**Paayal** – anklet
**Padma** – Goddess Lakshmi
**Padmaanjali** – full of lotus in the hand
**Padmahasta** – Goddess Lakshmi
**Padmaja** – Goddess Lakshmi
**Padmal** – lotus
**Padmalochan** – eyes like lotus
**Padmini** – lotus
**Pallavee** – creeper
**Pallavi** – new leaves
**Pallavine** – new leaves
**Pallavinee** – young shoot
**Palli** – lamp
**Pallikaa** – a small village
**Panchali** – draupadi

**Panchichallika** – doll
**Pankaj** – lotus
**Pankaajanee** – lotus plant
**Pankajnayanee** – lotus eyed
**Pankhuri** – petal
**Panna** – emerald
**Paral** – name of a flower
**Paramagnaa** – an ancient woman
**Paramita** – wisdom
**Parichiya** – introduction
**Paridhi** – realm
**Parimala** – a substance with fragrance
**Parimeetaa** – modest
**Parimitaa** – moderate

**Parmeshwary** – Goddess Durga

**Parnashri** – leafy beauty

**Parni** – leafy

**Parnikaa** – small leaf

**Parnitaa** – married woman

**Parthivi** – born from Earth

**Parvanee** – full Moon

**Parvati** – Goddess Durga

**Pavanee** – air, wind

**Pavani** – sacred

**Pavitraa** – pure

**Payaswini** – cow who gives milk

**Payoshmi** – name of the river

**Peeush** – nectar

**Piya** – beloved

**Poetika** – saffron

**Pooja** – worship

**Poonam** – full Moon

**Poorna** – complete

**Poornaashree** – full of beauty

**Poorvaa** – eastern

**Poorvi** – to east

**Poushah** – the month of Paush

**Praananjali** – joining two hands together to greet

**Praaneshvari** – beloved

**Praanjala** – leader

**Praayati** – advance

**Prabha** – lustre

**Prabhadra** – one who is shy

**Prabhava** – origin

**Prabhuti** – well

**Prabodhinee** – awakening

**Pracheetaa** – the soul

**Prachi** – east

**Prafullaa** – cheerful

**Pragati** – progress

**Pragnyee** – intelligent

**Pragya** – wisdom

**Praharsha** – happy person

**Prajanyaruchi** – the worship of knowledge

**Prakaashatee** – bright, shining

**Prakriti** – nature

**Pramila** – Arjun's wife

**Pramodini** – happy person

**Pranati** – prayer

**Pranavaa** – Young

**Pranjali** – simplicity

**Prasamitta** – composed

**Prashanshaa** – praise

**Prashanti** – peace

**Prateechi** – west

**Prathithi** – famous

**Pratibha** – genius

**Pratikshaa** – wait in hope

**Pratima** – statue

**Pratyangir** – form of Durga

**Praveena** – expert

**Pravritaa** – revolved

**Pradeepta** – glowing

**Prekshaa** – wise

**Prerna** – encouragement, inspiration

**Preyasi** – beloved

**Prithaa** – name of Kunti

**Prithvi** – the Earth

**Priti** – love

**Priya** – beloved

**Priyadarshni** – beautiful

**Priyal** – beloved

**Priyamvada** – soft spoken

**Priyanka** – dearest

**Priyankaree** – beloved

**Priyasha** – dearest

**Pujita** – worshipped

**Punitaa** – pure

**Punyaavati** – virtuous

**Purvaa** – east

**Pushpaangnaa** – delicate like flower

**Pushpajaa** – born of a flower

**Pushpangee** – delicate like flower

**Pushpanjali** – to pay respect

**Pushpitaa** – decorated with flower

**Pratishthaa** – glory

# R

**Rachnaa** – creation
**Raakhi** – full Moon
**Raatri** – night
**Rachitaa** – created
**Radha** – consort of Krishna
**Radhikaa** – Radha
**Ragaa** – musical notes
**Ragini** – a melody
**Rajnigandhaa** – name of a flower
**Rajitaa** – charming
**Rajni** – night
**Rajyashree** – wealth of kingdom
**Raksha** – defence
**Ramaa** – beautiful
**Rambha** – a celestial woman
**Ramneekaa** – beautiful
**Ramonaa** – protector
**Ramya** – champa
**Rangati** – classical song
**Ranjana** – pleasure
**Ranjeekaa** – one of the shruti
**Ranni** – night
**Rashmi** – Sun rays
**Rashmikaa** – a ray of light
**Ratee** – Goddess
**Rati** – pleasure
**Ratidaa** – giving pleasure
**Ratnaanjali** – red sandal
**Ratnamaalaa** – string of jewel
**Ratnavati** – the Earth
**Ravijaa** – daughter of the Sun, Yamuna
**Rekha** – line
**Renu** – Earth
**Renuka** – Earth

**Reshma** – silky
**Revatee** – prosperity
**Rewati** – Nakshatra
**Richa** – worship
**Rishikulyaa** –
  virtuous
**Rochana** – beautiful
**Rochanaa** – red lotus
**Rochanee** – beautiful
**Rochishaa** – light
**Rohini** – a Goddess
**Rokshadaa** –
  possessing light
**Roopa** – beauty
**Roopalekhaa** –
  streak of beauty
**Roopambaraa** –
  beautifully dressed
**Roopambaree** –
  beautifully dressed
**Rooparashmi** – rays
  of beauty

**Ruchaa** – lustre
**Ruchi** – desire
**Ruchiraa** – beautiful
**Rudhiraa** – one who
  is prosperous
**Rudra** – Goddess
  Durga
**Rudrana** – Goddess
  Parvati
**Rujulaa** – honest
**Rujusmitaa** – a
  person having a
  sober smile
**Rujusmriti** – a
  person having sober
  memory
**Rukmani** – jewel of
  gold
**Rupashree** –
  beautiful Lakshmi
**Rutumbharaa** – one
  who bears celestial
  truth

# S

**Saarangi** – a musical instrument

**Saarikaa** – woman, bird

**Saavitri** – wife of Satyavan

**Sadhnaa** – concentration

**Saadhvi** – a woman with high character

**Saloni** – beautiful

**Sambhavanaa** – probability

**Sameekshaa** – critical analysis

**Samishti** – group of all

**Sampadaa** – property

**Samtaa** – equality

**Sandhyaa** – evening

**Sangeetaa** – music

**Sapna** – dream

**Sanskriti** – culture

**Saras** – juicy

**Saraswati** – Goddess of learning

**Sargam** – seven notes of music

**Sarit** – river

**Sarojini** – lotus

**Sarpani** – snake (female)

**Saudamani** – lightning

**Saujanyaa** – kind

**Saumayaa** – beautiful

**Saveraa** – morning, light

**Seemaa** – limit

**Seemantini** – woman

**Shail** – mountain, rock

**Shailjaa** – Parwati

**Shailee** – mode of expression

**Shamlaa** – dark, evening, candle
**Shanivi** – pride
**Shanti** – peace
**Sharadaa** – a season, winter
**Shardaa** – Durga
**Sharikaa** – a bird (maina)
**Sharvari** – night
**Shashi** – Moon
**Shashikalaa** – art of Moon
**Shayama** – Radha
**Sheela** – behaviour
**Sheetal** – cool
**Shilpi** – a sculptor
**Shivika** – palki
**Shobha** – beauty
**Shradha** – respect
**Shravani** – full Moon day of Shravan
**Shruti** – listener
**Shubhrata** – white
**Shubra** – white
**Shukla** – Saraswati
**Shukti** – shell
**Shweta** – white

**Siddhi** – successfully completed
**Sindhusuta** – Goddess Lakshmi
**Sindooja** – Goddess Lakshmi
**Sindoori** – red colour, married
**Sitara** – star
**Smita** – polite laugh
**Smriti** – remembrance
**Sneh** – love
**Stuti** – praise
**Subhadra** – wife of Arjuna
**Subheeta** – ease
**Subhga** – beautiful
**Subhuti** – well behaved
**Subhodhini** – clever
**Sucharita** – well behaved
**Sucheta** – one with a very sharp mind
**Suchira** – eternity
**Sugandha** – with perfume

**Sugandhita** – a woman with good smell

**Sukeshi** – a woman with good hair

**Sukhda** – a woman who gives happiness

**Sukhyati** – fame

**Sukratee** – a person who does good deeds

**Sukriti** – good deeds

**Sulakshna** – lucky, with good character

**Sulbha** – which is available easily

**Sumantra** – good advice

**Sumati** – good advisor, intelligent

**Sumedha** – sensible

**Sumiran** – to remember

**Sumitra** – wife of Dashratha

**Sumukhi** – a woman with a beautiful face

**Sunanda** – delighted

**Sunandita** – joyful

**Sundari** – beautiful

**Suneelaa** – dark blue

**Suneeti** – good advice

**Sunena** – a girl with beautiful eyes

**Sunitaa** – well, beloved

**Sunitee** – good conduct

**Supriyaa** – much loved

**Suramyaa** – very beautiful

**Surangna** – wife of God

**Suratee** – remember

**Surbaalaa** – good singing girl

**Surabhi** – good smell, sandal wood

**Surdhirgikaa** – Mandakini

**Surdhuni** – Mandakini

**Suree** – wife of God

**Suruchi** – good taste

**Suryatanyaa** – river Yamuna

**Sushmaa** – very beautiful

**Sushobhitaa** – very beautiful

**Sushree** – very beautiful, rich

**Sutanu** – a woman with a beautiful body

**Suvidhaa** – ease

**Swadhurni** – Ganga

**Swaamini** – female preacher

**Swaati** – wife of Sun

**Swayamvaraa** – a woman who has selected her husband

# T

**Taapi** – name of the river

**Taapti** – name of the river

**Taarika** – a small actress

**Taarinee** – a raft

**Tamanna** – desire

**Tamasaa** – dark complexioned

**Tamasvini** – darkness

**Tandra** – fatigue

**Tanmaya** – fully absorbed

**Tanu** – delicate

**Tanu kesha** – delicate hair

**Tanujaa** – daughter

**Tanushree** – beautiful

**Tanveer** – delicate woman

**Tanya** – daughter

**Tapaswini** – a person who performs penance

**Tapasyaa** – penance

**Taapti** – Sun's daughter, a name of a river

**Taaraa** – star

**Taraanaa** – rythm

**Taralaa** – splendid

**Taralitaa** – shaking

**Taranee** – a ray of light

**Taranga** – wave

**Taranginee** – river

**Tarani** – boatr

**Tarannum** – melody

**Tareshwari** – parvati

**Tarini** – Goddess Parvati

**Tarini-tanayaa** – daughter of the Sun

**Tarlikaa** – shaking

**Tarpani** – a tree, river Ganges

**Tarulataa** – creeper

**Tarunee** – a young woman

**Tarunikaa** – young girl

**Tavishi** – earth, Durga, Indra's damsel

**Teertha** – holy place

**Tejasee** – lustre

**Tejashree** – lustrous beauty

**Tejasvitaa** – one who possesses light and splendour

**Tejata** – strong light

**Tejni** – a reed

**Tikshanarashmi** – the Sun

**Tikshnaa** – sharp

**Tilottamma** – name of a celestial woman

**Toral** – a folk heroine

**Tosha** – happy

**Toshitaa** – name of the demon

**Trilochanaa** – person with three eyes, mystique

**Trilokee** – three world

**Trinayani** – Goddess Durga

**Trinetra** – Goddess Durga

**Tripta** – satisfied

**Tripti** – satisfaction

**Trishalaa** – name of the mother of Lord Mahavira

**Trishna** – desire

**Triveni** – the three rivers

**Trushaa** – thirst

**Trushitaa** – desirous of profit

**Tuhina** – snow

**Tulasi** – basil plant

**Tullikaa** – brush

**Tungabhadraa** – name of the river

**Tushti** – satisfaction

**Twishaa** – lustre

**Twishi** – lustrous

# U

**Uchita** – proper
**Udasutaa** – Goddess Lakshmi
**Uddipti** – lighted
**Udit** – the rising Sun
**Ugra** – Goddess Kali
**Ugraa** – strong
**Ugraakali** – Goddess Durga
**Ugragandha** – fragrance
**Ugratejasa** – possessing great energy
**Ujaalaa** – light, luminous
**Ujilaa** – bright
**Ukti** – speech
**Ulhasinee** – cheerful person
**Uma** – Goddess Parvati
**Umang** – happiness, aspiration

**Unnati** – progress
**Upaasnaa** – worship
**Upaangana** – possessing intimate knowledge
**Urevijya** – victory of the Earth
**Urmikaa** – ring
**Urmilaa** – beautiful
**Uru** – big
**Uruchaksha** – big eyes
**Urvashi** – the celestial damsel
**Urvee** – Earth
**Urvijaa** – born of the Earth
**Usha** – dawn
**Usha Kiran** – the first ray of the Sun at dawn
**Usheetaa** – a person who dwells
**Ushmaa** – angry

**Ushnaa** – the hot season

**Utkalikaa** – seducive

**Utpalaa** – lotus, water lily

**Utprabha** – Sunlight

**Utprekshaa** – imagination

**Utsuraa** – twilight

**Uttamaa** – the chaste woman

**Uttra** – the wife of Abhimanyu, northward

# V

**Vaachyaa** – expressed

**Vaagdaa** – Goddess Saraswati

**Vaagdevi** – Goddess Saraswati

**Vaageshwari** – Goddess of speech

**Vaagheshwaree** – Goddess Durga

**Vaaka** – speech

**Vaamaa** – beautiful

**Vaamaakshi** – one who possesses beautiful eyes

**Vaamalochna** – fair eyed

**Vaani** – Goddess Saraswati

**Vaarangi** – one who possesses beautiful body

**Vaasanti** – youthful

**Vaasnaa** – desire, lust

**Vadhu** – bride

**Vahinee** – glowing

**Vaibhvi** – rich person

**Vaihaayasi** – aerial

**Vaijayanti** – a banner

**Vaijayantikaa** – a garland of pearl

**Vaijayantimalaa** – garland of Vaijayanti flower

**Vaishwaanaree** – omnipresent

**Vajra** – Goddess Durga

**Vajreshwari** – Buddhist Goddess

**Vallabhee** – beloved

**Vallakee** – musical instrument

**Vallaree** – Goddess Parvati

**Valli** – creeper

**Vama** – woman

**Vanaalikaa –** Sunflower

**Vanadevee –** Goddess of forest

**Vanamala –** garland of forest

**Vanamallikaa –** queen of the forest

**Vanasarojini –** the wild cotton plant

**Vanashree –** wealth of the wood

**Vandana –** adoration

**Vandanee –** worship

**Vandaneeyaa –** saluted

**Vanitaa –** woman

**Vanshalakshmi –** the wealth of the family

**Vanshikaa –** flute

**Vapusha –** a Goddess

**Varanganaa –** beautiful woman

**Varchaa –** power

**Vardaa –** granting boon

**Varinee –** a woman

**Varishaa –** rain

**Varnanaa –** description

**Varsha –** rain

**Varshikaa –** the dress of an actress

**Varshitaa –** rained

**Varunee –** consort of sea God

**Vasantaa –** spring

**Vasudaa –** the Earth

**Vashudha –** Earth

**Vasumatee –** a rich woman

**Vasumati –** the Earth

**Vasundhraa –** Earth

**Vatsalikaa –** affectionate

**Vatsalyaa –** motherly love

**Vavditaa –** a person who is praised by others

**Vedasmriti –** memory of the Veda

**Vedikaa –** altar

**Veena –** musical instrument

**Venee** – Krishna
**Veni** – a braided hair
**Venu** – flute
**Vetravati** – door keeper
**Vibhaa** – lustre, night
**Vibhaavaree** – night full of stars
**Vibhuti** – ashes
**Vidhatree** – Goddess
**Vidhu** – Moon
**Vidhulataa** – a streak of lightning
**Vidhyagauri** – Goddess of knowledge
**Vidhyut** – lightning
**Vidushi** – a scholar
**Vidyaa** – knowledge
**Vignyaapnaa** – request
**Vihangnee** – one who flies like a bird
**Vijaya** – Goddess Durga
**Vijayanti** – a celestial woman

**Vejetaa** – victorious
**Vikaasinee** – progressive
**Vikrantee** – powerful
**Vilaasinee** – graceful movements
**Vilochanaa** – the eyes
**Vimlaa** – clear
**Vinantikaa** – humble
**Vinanyaa** – humble
**Vinitaa** – Garuda's mother
**Vinati** – prayer
**Vincy** – winner
**Vinodnee** – joyous
**Vipulaa** – Earth
**Virachanaa** – arrangement
**Virajaa** – freedom from passion
**Vishakhaa** – without a branch
**Vishalakshi** – with large eyes
**Vishikhaa** – pin
**Vishvambhari** – the Earth

**Vitasta** – jhelum
 river
**Vivekaa** – wise
**Vivekini** –
 discriminating
**Viyogini** – one who is
 separated and is
 sad

**Vrataa** – fast
**Vrindaa** – basil
**Vritti** – temperament
**Vrutti** – existing
**Vyoma** – the sky
**Vyomikaa** – reside in
 the sky

# W-X-Y-Z

**Wahida** – beautiful
**Wamika** – Goddess Durga
**Wamila** – beautiful
**Yaachanaa** – an entreaty
**Yaamini** – night
**Yadugiri** – melukote hills
**Yajmadaya** – risen from sacred fire
**Yakshanganee** – river
**Yakshinee** – female Yaksha
**Yamabhaginee** – Yamuna river
**Yamavatee** – night
**Yami** – night
**Yamini** – night
**Yamuna** – river
**Yashaswati** – famous
**Yashaswinee** – famous mother

**Yashodha** – Krishna's mother
**Yashodhra** – buddha's wife
**Yashonidhi** – ocean of fame
**Yogini** – one who meditates
**Yogita** – achievements
**Yogmaya** – the magical power of Yoga
**Yojana** – planning
**Yoshitaa** – a girl
**Yugandhra** – Earth
**Yukti** – logic
**Yuti** – one who unites
**Yutika** – jasmine flower
**Yuvti** – a woman
**Zaheera** – expression
**Zareen** – golden
**Zarinaa** – queen
**Zeenat** – glory
**Zenia** – a flower
**Zohraa** – jupiter planet
**Zulekhaa** – beautiful

# OUR OTHER PUBLICATIONS

## ENGLISH IMPROVEMENT

## LANGUAGE SERIES

G-109   Learn Chinese through English
G-394   Chinese Made Easy
G-412   French Made Easy
G-439   German Made Easy

## BOOKS ON PUZZLES

G-86    Puzzles for the High IQ
G-87    Critical Thinking Puzzles
G-92    250 Challenging Puzzles
G-111   Challenging Science Puzzles
G-170   Challenging Math Puzzles
G-171   Great Picture Puzzles
G-247   Math Magic
G-289   Amazing Math Magic
G-292   Hard to Solve Math Puzzles
G-296   Mathemania
G-430   Challenging Brain Boosters

## BABY NAMES

G-46    Goodwill's Book of Baby Names
G-85    4500 Baby Names
G-116   10,000 Baby Names (in two colours)

## BOOKS ON IQ

G-16    Test Your IQ
G-22    Check Your IQ
G-23    How to Improve Your IQ
G-24    IQ for All
G-27    Better Your IQ
G-94    Take the IQ Challenge
G-200   Challenging IQ Tests

## BOOKS ON QUIZ

G-35    G.K. Quiz (Pocket size)
G-51    World Facts at a Glance
G-52    Do you Know

## ESSAY WRITING

## PALMISTRY, ASTROLOGY AND NUMEROLOGY

## GOODWILL'S SKILL BUILDERS

## PROJECTS / EXPERIMENTS

## RELIGION

## SPEECHES

## HEALTH AND FITNESS